The Quality of
Homelessness In Santa Cruz
1985-1992

by Paul A. Lee

Platonic Academy Press
Box 409
Santa Cruz, California 95061

Other books by Paul Lee

Florence the Goose 1992

Alan Chadwick and the Salvation of Nature 1992

The Meaning f Health by Paul Tillich
Introduction by Paul Lee

The Quality of Mercy
Homelessness In Santa Cruz 1985-1992

Designed by Robert Page
Electronic Composition Richard Curtis
In Adobe Janson Text
Printed and Bound by Publishers Press, Salt Lake City Utah,
On 70 lb. Husky Vellum Offset

To the memory of
Mitch Snyder, the national advocate for the homeless,
and to Jane Imler and Peter Carota, local inspirations
of civic virtue, in their concern for the homeless.

Contents

Preface

by Paul Lee

It is my wish to enter a personal word about helping someone in need. In 1976, I was a visiting lecturer at Emerson College, in Forest Row, England and spending weekends in London. One night, I went to dinner in a suburb of London. After dinner, my hosts dropped me off at a subway station to catch a train back to Kensington. It was terribly cold on the open platform and a strong wind was blowing. I was standing in front of a screen and heard a wracking cough, as though approximating a death rattle. After a few minutes, I could not endure this sound, what struck me as the sound of a man dying. I looked over the screen and there was a man lying on a bench, without covers, at the mercy of the elements, and obviously no where else to go. I glanced down the length of his body as I watched him heave convulsively from his coughing and there saw a large clumsy black shoe—oversized. He was a club foot. This dying cripple struck me with such force I thought I must take him home with me and care for him for the night, lest, leaving him there, he would be dead by morning. The train arrived, I boarded it, and went home alone. I have never forgiven myself for not acting on my response to this man's plight, although, now, after six years of working for the homeless, I have at least done something to make up for it.

Jesus answered,

Foxes have their holes, the birds their roosts;
but the Son of Man has nowhere to lay his head.

Luke 9: 58

Acknowledgements

I want to thank Page Smith, my faithful friend in all times but especially in times of trouble, for his devotion to the cause of homelessness; Paul Pfotenhauer, for his help and friendship in a time of need that has extended over the years; and Fred Gray, Andrew Morin, Lynne Basehore, Karen Gillette, Shana Ross and Paddy Long, who have stood on the front line.

When looking for the source of the quote used for the title, Adelaide De Menil referred me to the *Merchant of Venice*; Ted Carpenter found the quote and after reading an early draft offered advice on some changes in the text, for which I am grateful. Congressman Leon Panetta sent a large packet of valuable and useful information on government and public studies on the homeless and available sources of funding. The bibliographies were especially helpful. Peter John provided me with the German reference for Tillich's article: *"The Philosophy of Social Work"*, and he sent to me the article by Paul Ricoeur on *"The Golden Rule"*, which I treasure. Within weeks after receiving the article, Lynne Basehore, the Director of our Homeless Garden Project, won "The Golden Rule" Award, from the J. C. Penny Foundation, for her volunteer work.

Hillevi Wyman proofread the text with a finetooth comb and offered a number of invaluable suggestions; Elizabeth Spafford helped select the photographs; Rose at Lasersmith formatted the text and prepared it for publication; and Fred Gray hooked up my new Mac Scanner and entered the photographs after helping with the text. Omar Liripio obtained an additional hard disc and assisted in technical matters. I am indebted to them for their help.

I used a book I had published with Jack Stauffacher—*The Meaning of Health*, by Paul Tillich—as my model for the design and Jack lent his expert hand to the final format. I owe the fulfillment of my love of type and paper and text design to Jack Stauffacher and the Greenwood Press, of San Francisco.

Robert Page took over the design of the book at the final stage and with his fine sense of style made it what it is today.

The Quality of Mercy was composed on a Mac SE, one of the loves of my life, with an H-P ink-jet printer and a Mac Scanner. It was a thrill to be able to incorporate photos and newspaper articles directly into the book with this terrific tool. It makes desk top text-editing for publishing, a realized dream.

All the others, too many to name here, who have been so helpful and unsparing in their contribution to the homeless crisis in Santa Cruz are known to themselves and carry our thanks and gratitude.

Introduction

Page Smith

In *The Quality Of Mercy*, Paul Lee has combined a simple narrative of the experience of one small American community with the homeless with a larger moral and ethical issue of homelessness in America and, indeed, the world. It is an experience we share. In the stories he tells about our friendships with the homeless he helps us see them as human beings, brothers and sisters, in need of help and, above all, of love.

The rise of the Welfare State encouraged us to think that such issues as poverty and homelessness could be taken care of by the State through a corps of trained experts called social workers. The rest of us could then go about our respective businesses free of any qualms of conscience about the condition of the less fortunate members of our society. They, we were confident, were being adequately provided for through the appropriate agencies, federal, state and local. It is proof of the distinction Tillich draws between true charity and charity by proxy.

The fact is that we dare not break the connection between the assumed relatively prosperous (and generally reform-minded) middle class and those in need. As *The Quality of Mercy* makes clear, social service agencies cannot do the job for the rest of us.

The social services, for several generations, have attracted superior men and women with a mission for service to others; they have been absorbed (and often frustrated to the point of despair) in caste welfare bureaucracies where the spirit languishes and often dies under the sheer weight of "cases" and "case loads". Small wonder. Social workers are charged with doing our work for us under the most difficult circumstances. Underpaid and overworked they cannot, provide the human responses, the care and love, without which charity becomes a curse rather than a blessing.

Some years ago, the journalist, Peter Marin, wrote a famous essay entitled: "Helping and Hating the Homeless". In that essay, Marin explored our ambivalent feelings about the homeless. Among other things, we are constantly trying to make what are often excessively subtle (and irrelevant) distinctions between the "deserving" and the "undeserving" homeless, those who want to work but are down on their luck and just need a helping hand to get back in the "main stream", and those who are "bums", beggars and ne'er-do-wells, etc. who should be chased out of town, thrown in jail, systematically harrassed by the authorities and in other ways, many of them illegal, persuaded to move on.

I think anyone who has worked for the homeless knows that the reality is usually too complex to yield to such superficial analyses. There are wounded hearts and souls whom we dare not approach in a patronizing or condescending spirit. James Russell Lowell, one of our best (and most neglected) poets, wrote, in the middle of the last century, *The Vision of Sir Launfal*, the most famous line of which is "What is so rare as a day in June?" The poem is about Sir Launfal's quest for the Holy Grail and the salvation of his soul. Attired in his "richest mail", splendidly mounted, he sets forth from his castle. At the gateway a leper begs for alms, a figure so abject that the knight's flesh beneath his armor begins to "shrink and crawl". Years later, when he returns from his arduous and futile search, worn down by time and disappointment, he encounters once more the leper, now revealed as the Christ Figure, the suffering servant, whom he had ridden by so contemptuously at the beginning of his journey.

The homeless, as the poorest of the poor, test our capacity for charity/love, often it must be said, quite severely. Is it measured and conditional, hedged about with cautious reservations or is it generous and wholehearted?

There are practical considerations. There is a vast "welfare bureaucracy" staffed by many able and dedicated individuals, but bound by innumerable rules, designed, we are constantly reminded, "to protect the tax-payer". To the welfare establishment, we seem merely muddled do-gooders, without the requisite "training" or "degrees", amateurs, in short. To those amateurs committed to helping the homeless, the professionals often seem a major impediment, forced as the professionals are to deal with cases.

Yet the fact is that we must work together. We each have some essential elements to contribute to, I fear, not a solution to the eternal problem of poverty and homelessness, but to a mitigation of it's harshest aspects.

Although much, much, remains to be done, here and elsewhere, Santa Cruz has made, with, to be sure, various blunders and errors, a good beginning. This is the story of that beginning. It's most valuable contribution is that rather than treating the issue of homelessness in Santa Cruz as a "social problem" or as an "economic problem" or as a "political problem", it will not let us forget that it is, above all, a moral issue that has to do with the most profound values of life itself.

The quality of mercy is not strain'd,—
    It droppeth as the gentle rain from heaven
    Upon the place beneath: it is twice blest,—
    It blesseth him that gives, and him that takes...

Portia
Merchant of Venice IV.1[1]

Chapter One
Homelessness In Santa Cruz

Homelessness is not easy to think about. In fact, one would rather do something about it than think about it. It is the tradition of the pragmatic American way. The plight of the homeless demands action more than thought. Nevertheless, there is much to think about in assessing the homeless and many questions come to mind after working with the homeless for the last six years. Why has there been a growing population of homeless every year since the late 1970s? What has happened in our country that people lack shelter and have nowhere to go at night when it turns cold and dark?

Isn't the right to shelter one of the basic human rights not to be denied anyone?

Is a philosophy of homelessness possible to develop and is this a task this book should attempt to fulfill, even though, as Tillich says, in his address on the "Philosophy of Social Work", appended to the end of this book, beyond anyone's power to do so?

I can't say I develop a philosophy of homelessness in this book, but I do raise some philosophical issues and the basic theme of the book—"the quality of mercy"—was given to me as a title before I knew what it meant in terms of the discussion developed here. I came to realize that it was a great phrase for an ethic of abundance, in this case spiritual abundance, where the measure you give is the measure you receive, not in the sense of *quid pro quo.* No, quite the contrary, more in the sense of a lack of measure, where the phrase—go for broke—comes to mind. We were willing to risk it and we were rewarded by the success of our programs. It has been as simple as that.

We didn't mind taking on something beyond our power like the cause of homelessness in Santa Cruz because there were so many who were willing to help. We now have a community of people involved in the task of alleviating the misery of homelessness in Santa Cruz.

In our work with the homeless, I have been guided by a saying I had already taken to heart as a major statement, even before the homeless issue came up. It was a saying waiting for me to apply it. It provided me with food for thought in terms of a philosophy of social work even though it is a statement that seems to argue that the infinite dignity and worth of a human being is now so eroded that it has to be formulated in an almost crazily exaggerated way just to make the point.

The principle was formulated around 1910, by Josef Popper-Lynkeus, a Viennese social reformer and scientist, who was a figure of great inspiration for many who knew him, such as Einstein and others. Freud revered him and wrote an essay about him, but didn't want to meet him lest the reality disappoint the image.

Popper-Lynkeus called his statement *a basic principle of a moral social philosophy:*

> *"When any individual, of however little account but one who does not deliberately imperil another's existence, disappears from the world, without or even against his or her will, this is a far more important happening than any political or religious or national occurrence, or the sum total of the scientific and artistic and technical advances made throughout the ages by all the peoples of the world.*
>
> *Should anybody be inclined to regard this statement as an exaggeration, let them imagine the individual concerned to be themself or their best beloved. Then they will understand and accept it."*

These two paragraphs are deceptively short thanks to their terse pungency. They demand a very close reading in order to grasp their meaning. What is meant, for instance, by "disappearing from the world"? It is a term close to Paul Tillich's remark about "feeling unnecessary", a prelude to despair and hopelessness. In his remarkable book: *The Courage To Be*, Tillich mentions how people in the Great Depression thought they had *ceased to exist* because they were unemployed. Having a job in America means existence itself. Not having a job means disappearing—ceasing to exist. You see it in the photographs of the faces of men sitting on park benches in the Depression, in the depths of despair, where they are absent from themselves. They have disappeared.[2]

A situation was to occur within a few decades that would exemplify what Popper-Lynkeus meant by 'disappearance'. He anticipated the 'disappearance of the Jews' in the Holocaust of Nazi Germany. The Final Solution, organized by Hitler and Himmler, was for the Jews to disappear. What was meant was extermination. This has to be the criterion, or the reference point, for the meaning of the word— 'disappearance'. At the same time, millions of people 'disappeared' in the terror of the Russian purge under Stalin. In more recent history, there are those who 'disappeared' in Argentina and in Chile; those who 'disappeared' in China, during the Cultural Revolution; those who 'disappeared' in the South during the Civil Rights struggle; those who 'disappear' every day, somewhere in the world, of however little account, without or even against their will.

Homelessness is just such an issue of "disappearing from the world". The homeless have disappeared right in front of our face. There they are, lying in a doorway of a store or business, on the sidewalk, in a vacant lot, abandoned and forgotten. Although this is seldom seen in Santa Cruz, where it is a criminal offense to be caught 'sleeping' in a public place, it is a common scene in various areas of big cities, such as San Francisco, New York, London, Amsterdam, Lisbon.

What else can "disappearing from the world" mean, in this case, where a human being has become a piece of refuse? Against this, Popper-Lynkeus poses the most exaggerated statement in the history of human thought, in order to dramatize the juxtaposition: the infinite worth and dignity of a human person against the whole sum of cultural achievements by all the peoples of the world. Not even *this sum* is equal to *one person* who has disappeared!

And then he says: if you think this is an exaggeration, (when it is the greatest exaggeration ever formulated), think of that person as yourself or your best beloved, to drive the point home, in what is known in philosophy as an *argumentum ad hominem.*

The idea of the infinite value and worth of a human being has eroded in this century, a century of world wars and wholesale slaughter of human lives through genocide. Popper-Lynkeus anticipated this in his odd formulation. He had to put the issue on a personal basis: think of yourself or your best beloved.

What do you value?, he wants to know. He says a person is valued on a scale from zero to infinity, which seems to imply that the value of a human being is a mystery. A human being is of incomparable worth. "Shall I compare thee to a summer's day?"

He takes umbrage with a famous German art historian who had the gall to say that all of the deaths of Greek slaves were not worth one sculpting of Phidias. That made Popper-Lynkeus mad. He proposed that the art historian suffer slavery for a few decades and then retire with an apartment at the Louvre where he could look at sculptings and think of what he said now that he has some personal understanding of it.

What would you do if there was a fire in the Louvre?, he asks. Would you save the people or the paintings? If an angel of death were to ask for the lives of two common day laborers to save Michaelangelo or Raphael or Shakespeare would you give them up for sacrifice? No, of course not.

I had a strange experience in this regard. I was at the Museum of Modern Art at an exhibition of the late paintings of Cezanne, one of my favorite artists. I turned from one painting and looked at a young woman who was a Punk, with pins in her cheeks and garish hair and I had to admit that she was of greater value than the Cezanne, another order of value. I know the difference between a painting and a person.

I think of Wittgenstein when I think of this saying of Popper-Lynkeus. He lost his sense of human decency in the trenches of the First World War and never again wore a tie lest it be thought he could resume his place in the company of decent men. It was a symbolic moment for this century's great philosopher when the value and worth of a human being is lost along with the sense of human decency.

Paul Tillich, as a chaplain at the front, in the same war, heard the screams of his men calling on "*Lieber Gott*"; their screams went unanswered.

Eugen Rosenstock-Huessy, in the trenches of Verdun, thought of the breakdown of Western culture and sketched out in his mind his great work: *Out of Revolution*, where he quotes Lefebvre: "Shall dogs and horses scent a thunderstorm and man and woman not sense the breakdown of a social order that has lasted a thousand years?."

With this breakdown in Western culture came the decline of the value and meaning of humanity itself. Human beings were cannon fodder, pawns in the great wars of hostile nation states, bent upon self-destruction. And then came Hitler to fill the void.

No wonder that Popper-Lynkeus had to define the value and worth of a person negatively, when seen against the sum total of cultural achievements; one person is worth more than the sum of it all, when that person is allowed to disappear; the value re-appears in the most absurdly exaggerated formulation of that value.

Does this account for the impact the homeless make on us as we go our way in our effort to ignore them, denying the moment, in the course of our lives, when we are called upon to meet the plight of a human being in need? What we deny, in our refusal to help them, we deny in ourselves: a sense of human decency.

It may be that we have reversed the Popper-Lynkeus equation: the homeless have no worth at all because we have so little sense of the value of ourselves and our best beloved. "So what?", we say, almost one hundred years later: "I'm not worth much, my best beloved is only worth a little more, to me, and therefore the homeless are nothing!"

The sense of the infinite worth of human beings, as such, ourselves included, is no longer generally recognized or affirmed. Life is cheap and easily expendable. We have lost our sense of human decency which depends on such a valuation of infinite worth. Then Tillich's "law of listening love", no longer applies, because it cannot be summoned or counted on.

But this is not true.

Against all measures of scepticism and cynicism, people step forward to respond spontaneously to the depth of human need and something happens. It is almost impossible to plan and difficult to predict. It happens. And when it does, one gets a sense of "the means of grace", still operating in our midst and the original meaning of the words: *caritas* and *agape*.. Where it comes from is to be trusted.

This has been our experience in working with the homeless. We went into the effort without a plan, with little experience, in response to an emergency need. We found countless others who were willing to help, often without even calling on them to help—they appeared: with blankets, with food, with appliances, with clothing, with money, whatever was needed. There were vast untapped resources of care and concern in the Santa Cruz community that rallied to the cause to refute the prevailing notion that the homeless were unwelcome and should leave, especially if they wanted to escape a beating at the hands of the police.

One of the motives for writing this book is to thank all of you who have contributed to alleviating the plight of the homeless and who have helped make Santa Cruz a place where the quality of mercy is not strained but abundantly evident in the generosity of those who have contributed to the cause.

Shakespeare was right when he wrote that "the quality of mercy is not strained", because he knew of an ethic of abundance, where, according to the measure you give, *more* will be given to you, heaped up, spilling over. The lack of measure is the good measure:

"...give, and it will be given to you; good measure, pressed down, shaken together, running over, will be put into your lap. For the measure you give will be the measure you get back." Luke 6:38.

The Apostle Paul touches this theme, in his inimitably paradoxical language when he speaks about how Jesus as the Christ, who was rich, was made poor for us that we might be rich.

> *For you know the grace of our Lord Jesus Christ,*
> *that though he was rich, yet for your sake he*
> *became poor, so that by his poverty you might*
> *become rich.*

He goes on to address the riddle of inequality expressing the theme of abundance even when there doesn't seem to be enough.

> *And in this matter I give my advice: it is best*
> *for you now to complete what a year ago you*
> *began not only to do but to desire, so that your*
> *readiness in desiring it may be matched by your*
> *completing it out of what you have. For if the*
> *readiness is there, it is acceptable according*
> *to what a man has, not according to what he has*
> *not. I do not mean that others should be eased and*
> *you burdened, but that as a matter of equality*
> *your abundance at the present time should supply*
> *your want, that there may be equality. As it is,*
> *written, "He who gathered much had nothing over,*
> *and he who gathered little had no lack."*

When I read this personal word of Paul to the Church at Corinth, I was perplexed by the quote, where Paul refers to Exodus 16:18. I looked it up and lo and behold it was like learning a secret, the code word for which was "manna".

> *"And when the dew had gone up, there was on*
> *the face of the wilderness a fine, flake-like*
> *thing, fine as hoarfrost on the ground. When*
> *the people of Israel saw it, they said to one*
> *another, "What is it?" For they did not know*
> *what it was. And Moses said to them, "It is*
> *bread which the Lord has given you to eat.*
> *This is what the Lord has commanded: 'Gather*
> *of it, every man of you, as much as he can eat;*
> *you shall take an omer apiece, according to the*
> *number of the persons whom each of you has*
> *in his tent.'"*
>
> *And the people of Israel did so; they gathered,*
> *some more, some less. But when they measured*
> *it with an omer, he that gathered much had*
> *nothing over, and he that gathered little had*
> *no lack; each gathered according to what he*
> *could eat."*

A recipe of sorts for manna is even given. It tastes like coriander seed pounded into flour mixed with honey and baked. I thought of making manna cakes and distributing them at the Free Meal some afternoon. The homeless would say: "what is it?"

This is the theme of the book—this abundance the homeless reveal. It is what I have learned over the last six years. It is the moral of my story.

We have been guided by another saying, attributed to Simone Weil, the famous French philosopher who died of self-imposed starvation in her despair over the suffering of the Second World War:

"Learn how to give as if you were begging."

Derelict, from the Latin: derelictus

forsaken, abandoned, deserted, without a guardian
guilty of dereliction of duty; delinquent, failure,
cessation, fainting
a vessel abandoned at sea
reprehensible abandonment or neglect

The word "derelict" cuts both ways—the population of bums and vagrants who are the derelicts, and our being derelict in our duty to them. We turned the word over and over in our minds according to these two meanings. We thought of being derelict in our duty to derelicts. How about that for coming to the end of your rope? We figured it meant changing a community attitude on the homeless: from "troll-busters" to supporters of a human conservation society.

When we started, we had nothing in hand, just our concern. We had no money, outside of what was in our pockets; we had no resources, beyond ourselves and our friends; we had no experience with working with the homeless, although Page Smith and I had worked with the jobless, in the William James Work Company, a nonprofit community service corporation we started in the 1970s, after our departure from the university. But then the situation was not so desperate. The word 'homeless' was never used. People were simply looking for some employment, short-term, part-time. Pick-up work. Before we closed down the Work Company we had found thirty thousand part-time jobs for people, not a bad record for a couple of loafers.

Now that we are six years into the homeless work, we have to deal with budgets amounting to millions of dollars in the five programs we are associated with. Given these figures, I started to think about the homeless as a new field for the entrepreneur. I even coined a term as a pun— "entropy nerds"— to characterize the new economic type involved with homelessness.

Entropy:
1. a thermodynamic measure of the amount of energy unavailable for useful work in a system undergoing change,

2. a measure of the degree of disorder in a system: entropy always increases and available energy diminishes in a closed system, as the universe,

3. in information theory, a measure of the information content of a message evaluated as to its uncertainty.

The first definition expresses the general view of the homeless—they are a drain. They represent energy unavailable for useful work. Therefore, they represent a degree of disorder, according to the second definition. It is our view that this so-called disorder, this chaos, can be turned to advantage, when the energy is put to work.

Then the third meaning comes into play—the *uncertainty* in the information becomes a new message with new meaning, as when a chronic alcoholic, who is homeless, goes on the wagon and becomes an important member of the staff of the Homeless Garden Project.

Nerd:
a person regarded as contemptibly dull, unsophisticated, ineffective.

From *entropynerds* to *entrepreneurs* has become our goal and battle cry, with every homeless person regarded as a fund of untapped potential. All it takes is a change of perspective, a gestalt switch, where the victim is transformed into a resource, and becomes a valuable member of a project, rather than a liability and a waste. After all, the homeless are bearers of dignity and worth, just like you and me. The victim can become a victor through a quirk of fate, an intervening opportunity, where untapped potential is given a chance to disclose itself.

The homeless, it turns out, are just as enterprising as anyone else in our society. All you have to do is turn this prospect, this possibility, to advantage. Where there is no ostensible hope, hope can be summoned. Hope can even take you by surprise, when you least expect it.

What seemed like a drain on energy and an impossible task was just the opposite—a new challenge to develop opportunities for people to escape from desperation and hopelessness. In fact, so many opportunities are possible, if the conditions are right and the imagination is there to propose new projects; and, according to our experience, the conditions are easy to establish. All you need is a little bluff, the outstanding quality of American pragmatism, where the proof is in the pudding.

We saw just that in the effort to organize the Cedar Street Shelter. The talent and ability were there, within the group, in the shelter. The homeless, themselves, had the ability to organize and run the place. All we had to do was call upon it, blow on it like a spark and it would ignite into a meaningful program and a community unto itself with its own sense of comraderie and morale. This was our experience in deferring to the homeless in the operation of the Cedar Street Shelter.

We had the same experience with the Interfaith Satellite Shelter. The homeless run it themselves in terms of our monitor program—they keep order and see to it that things run smoothly and peacefully. The best example of this spontaneous ability to run a project, where the talent simply surfaces, is the Free Meal Program, under Karen Gillette, where the homeless, themselves, run the show, providing a free meal for up to 150 people a night, seven days a week.

This is the story of our work with the homeless since the opening of the Cedar Street Shelter in 1985. It is a progress report to the people of Santa Cruz, who have been an enormous help, in a time of trouble and need, with financial and moral support. Although this is a progress report, it is written as a memoir. I have narrated what I have experienced and what I have learned as a result of getting involved in the homeless issue in 1985. My views are not necessarily shared by anyone else. I chose to tell the story from my point of view, even though I had help from Page Smith, Paul Pfotenhauer, Fred Gray, Andrew Morin, Karen Gillette,

Lynne Basehore, Bill Tracey and Judy Schwartz. But they are not responsible for the way I have told it. This is what has been accomplished; it is our interest to give you an accounting of it; and it is our chance to say thank you for your support and encouragement.

"I am done with great things and big plans, great institutions and big success. And I am for those tiny invisible loving human forces that work from individual to individual, creeping through the crannies of the world like so many rootlets, or like the capillary oozing of water, yet which, if given time, will rend the hardest monuments of human pride."

William James

Chapter Two
The Imler Fast and the Cedar Street Shelter

In the winter of 1985, Jane Imler, a resident of Santa Cruz, inspired by the example of Mitch Snyder, the national advocate for the homeless, working in Washington, D.C., made famous for his fasting in behalf of the homeless, announced that she was going to fast to the death unless someone opened a public shelter for the homeless in Santa Cruz. There was little interest in the threat. The response of the City Council, at the time, was, well, die then. I took it to heart and was bothered by it. I could not tolerate the notion that I had to take onto my conscience the death of a woman in my town who was making an appeal for the homeless no one was willing to act upon. A spontaneous response was demanded, if that is not a contradiction in terms.

So I asked my colleague and Co-Director of the William James Association, Page Smith, to consider opening a shelter as a new project of the Association. We had been doing community work since leaving the university in 1972 and we had turned to other concerns over the years and needed a new project to continue our work together.

We had been inspired by the example of Peter Carota, who had opened the first public food program for the homeless—St. Francis Kitchen—so we invited Peter to attend our next Board of Directors' meeting and advise us on opening a shelter. After that meeting we began looking for a prospective site. It struck us that the auditorium at the welfare building (Human Resources Agency) on Emeline Street, empty at night, was a decently warm and neutral space to provide a place for the homeless to lie down and sleep. There was an adjoining cafeteria. And, after all, it was the very agency that was supposed to help people in need like the homeless. We would organize it and run it.

We made the proposal to the Director of Human Resources. It was enough to make her squirm; she somewhat politely told us it was impossible. We asked why. She gave us a list of reasons, all of them skimpy, as far as we were concerned. She didn't seem to understand that we were going to open a shelter for the homeless. One of the reasons for refusing our request had to do with adding a door for security, not an insurmountable obstacle. We were even willing to pay for the door. We asked our friend, Roy Rydell, an architect, and a member of the Board of the William James Association, to investigate the matter and advise accordingly. He made it obvious it was no big deal and drew up the plan. We easily dealt with the other reasons for not letting us do it.

The Director suggested we find a place in downtown Santa Cruz and the County would pay the rent, just as long as it was some miles from the welfare complex. We decided it would be easier. We found an empty former family sauna, on Cedar Street, in downtown Santa Cruz, with nice little cells for sleeping (the women we would serve could have those, we figured, affording them some privacy) and a nice accommodatingly large room with a rug on the floor for the men. There were showers. We rented it. We were in the homeless business. We were called "shelter providers". We called it: "The Cedar Street Shelter".

The City had a fit. We had circumvented the permit process, something we didn't know about in the first place. The County could open a shelter without a permit from the City and that's what happened. We had to open a shelter and we had to do it fast to get Jane Imler off her fast. The County CAO—George Newall—took the heat. City Council members distinguished themselves by making stupid comments about our situation. They were going to deny us the $5,000 they had voted to give us thinking we would be going into the Emeline County Welfare Auditorium and therefore out of their area. It was the first indication that they were not nice guys and that any interest in the homeless was idle talk. So much for the liberalism of that ilk. They even had the gall to call themselves "Progressives".

Jane Imler, already in the hospital, ended her fast on the first day our doors were opened. She showed up on the first night to enjoy her first bowl of soup. Soon it was Christmas. Everyone got a pair of socks and we sang Christmas carols and had cookies and punch. It was terrific!

Then came the horrendous winter storms in a season of storms that wreaked havoc that year. Mud slides. The San Lorenzo River ready to overflow its banks. We huddled in and hunkered down to provide a space for everyone who came to the door. There were regulations, of course, and limitations in terms of occupancy based on fire laws. We got angry letters from "the authorities", complaining bitterly about exceeding our limit, which was erroneously figured at 25, a misreading of our space and the fire regulations. We thought: "let *them* come down during a storm and stand at the door and turn the homeless away". Attitudes like that earn you a bad reputation with the people in charge, who, we came to believe the hard way, were paid to hinder our efforts and anyone else, like ourselves, outside of the system, intent on helping the homeless. We were regarded as amateurish meddlers who had no business interfering in the professional realm of social work.

Page Smith determined the management plan. He thought he was organizing Cowell College all over again, only this time it was downtown with the homeless. No one of our homeless clients struck us as any crazier or further out there than some of the students we had to deal with in the mid-60s at UCSC, so it was a kind of homeless college *in nuce*. Page wanted someone to sleep there every night to act as a steadying influence, the beginning of our monitor system. I had a nice spare pecanwood bed I brought down to use for our monitors. We either rotated between Page and myself, or recruited someone from the community. We were delighted when the Mayor—Mike Rotkin—slept there one night. After all, he was an avowed Marxist and therefore sympathetic with the lumpen-proletariat.

I couldn't stand sleeping there at night. The snoring and the coughing and the farting kept me awake all night long. Page thought he was back in the army and slept like a Major. I had a hard time with a woman who had fits all night long. She would turn in a circle and cry out in a plaintive whine: "oh help me, oh help me". Her shuffle had a certain design to it. The thought passed my mind that she was acting. She was doing this godawful ritual just to keep me awake and to awaken others. I got up and went out to tell her she had to stop or leave. She was keeping everyone awake. O.K., if that wasn't true, she might wake someone up besides me. She left. She got dressed and got on her bicycle and went out into the night. It happened to be storming. I went back to bed. I thought: "I went to Harvard Divinity School to drive that poor woman out into the stormy night?"

I decided to befriend her. She became my favorite homeless person. I learned her name. I gave her my wife's bicycle when her bicycle was stolen. It was a very nice Raleigh. I gave her my daughter's bicycle when she told me the Raleigh was stolen. She kept her stuff in my parent's garage next door to me. She collected stuff—a piano, a loom, a wind-surfer outfit, complete with sails, jewelry, and bags and bags of stuff. She called one night and said she was going to San Jose. She was going to move there. She asked if I could bring her stuff—this was when there were only about a dozen big duffle bags— down to the bus depot. I did. The next night she called and said she wasn't going to San Jose after all. Would I come down and get her stuff and put it back in the garage? I did. The next night she called and said she was going after all and would I.... I did. The next night when she called, I said: "O.K., Jean, now I'm not going to do this again."

I visited her in the hospital when she had a leg infection. I took her to the hospital when she needed medication. She was a great example of someone you think can't make it for a day and years later, there she is on the phone: "Oh, Dr. Lee, I'm so glad to talk to you." She sounded like Mr. Bill on the old "Saturday Night Live" shows. We developed a continuing friendship. I thought I could make one unconditional commitment to one homeless person, so that no matter what transpired I would take it in stride. I was always glad to see her and she was always glad to see me. We had a kind of pact.

There were a number of examples like that, unique friendships that grew out of the shelter. We figured if we could trust them they would trust us and so we left it up to them to manage their own affairs.

The management of the shelter, in the hands of the homeless, demonstrated to us what we had hoped—they could organize themselves better than we could and the less we imposed any outside authority or discipline the better. It was the William James Work Company all over again. There were no incidents of any major significance in the months we were in operation. The manager in charge might get drunk one night and disqualify himself, appointing his successor, but that was the extent of it.

One night, one guy acted up and became aggressive and rather wild and threatening. Miraculously, as though he manifested himself just to deal with it, Paddy Long appeared on the sidewalk, a lay brother in a Roman Catholic order, with a history of experience with the homeless. He knew exactly what to do, just as we had reached the end of our rope and were about to call the cops. The guy calmed down as Paddy and I drove him over to the mental ward at Dominican and checked him in and that was that. Paddy was to continue to work with us through all of our efforts and proved to be an invaluable friend and advisor always on the ready to contribute whatever was needed.

I remember the little punk mick kid with his pet rats on either shoulder the day we opened. We all acted as if we couldn't see the rats. At least I did. It was more than I could cope with. Dogs, maybe. Cats, maybe. But rats!? I acted like I didn't see them. They would invariably hiss in a rasping rat-like gasp whenever I went near the kid. Sometimes he would hold them up in my face as I passed him and they would hiss: "can't see us, huh?" There were always little rat turds to clean up in the morning when I swept the room. I didn't care. I felt like Luther's maid with the broom sweeping to the glory of God. One day he rolled over on one of the rats when asleep, or it fell off his shoulder and broke it's neck. Anyhow, one of them was dead. He spent the day weeping over his dead rat. The dead one, I was happy to note, I could see.

Page Smith's favorite was Shiloh Superfly. Page has this bohemian side to him, typical of some academics. He was fond of the "Oily Scarf Wino Band", he and his wife, Eloise, discovered on the streets of Los Angeles. They used to bring them up to Santa Cruz to play at parties. The band would get loaded and sleep on the lawn. I thought, "what a party favor"!

If there was anything that prepared me for working with the homeless, it was getting to know the "Oily Scarf Wino Band".

I shared Page's affinity for the down and out. Shiloh, of course, was a biblical expert and knew the precise passages from scriptures that made the homeless the most spiritually advanced people in the history of the world, or Western culture, or at least Santa Cruz. Page would shake his head in a kind of bewildered appreciation that we had a prophet in our midst who could recite or write out the sayings of Jeremiah or Ezekiel and bring one to tears. It made up for the rats.

Shiloh was featured in our documentary television account of the shelter—"Voices of the Homeless"—opening with a beautiful prayer. We edited out the part that came at the end— he was praying for later hours in the shelter on Friday so he could watch "Friday Night Video" and rock and roll.

One guy—Fred Fetter—who looked like his name, a roly poly fellow with an alcoholic blear, who had been one of the shelter staff, decided he was going to hitch-hike down to San Diego and re-join the Merchant Marines. Page and I were at the Catalyst, a local restaurant and rock and roll showplace, on a sandwich break one night when Fred came over and asked if he could buy us a pitcher of beer. We said, "sure". He sat down saying that it was like sitting down with Clark Gable (Page) and Ernest Hemingway (me). You can't beat that for openers. We said, "What's your story, Fred? Tell us something about yourself." "Well", he said, "I was a mercenary soldier in Zimbabwe". "No kidding!" "Yep". "Tell us something about that". "Well. when we were supposed to be paid after our tour of duty they only had money for half of us, so they rented a plane, put half of the guys in it and when it was high in the sky blew it up."

We wished him good luck and said goodbye to Fred Fetter.

One of the nicest aspects was the turn-around in the business community surrounding the shelter. Because there was no fuss, no muss, no untoward incident to cause a ruckus, they quickly became partisans of the cause, rather than detractors, and we welcomed their support. The neighbor bagel baker gave us left-over bagels. It undermined the notion that one is in favor of a shelter for the homeless as long as it isn't in one's neighborhood. After all, the homeless had to leave at 8:00 am and could not come back until 5:00 pm; as it was dark during those hours, in the wintertime, they were practically invisible.

Then came the discovery of the demonic. I had learned the concept from my teacher, Paul Tillich. He actually claimed to have rediscovered it for modern theology, in the 1930s, in Germany. He had a great way of formulating its meaning: "a structure of destruction". The demonic hit and it was tough. It drove us apart, those of us who were working together; gossip and back-biting is a great symptomatic symbol of it. Friends fall out with friends and colleagues with colleagues. A disruptive atmosphere appeared and tempers flared. I was amazed that what I had learned in the dry books of theology was now being played out in front of my face. The demonic, fortunately, was kept at bay and after a few attacks we recovered and seemed to be immune, although I maintained a sense of it from then on. When people are down and out they seem to be at the mercy of the demonic more than others, although it may only be more visible or evident. It reminded me of the meaning of the wrath of God, where one's vitality is directed against oneself in a syndrome of self-destruction.

We appealed to the community for financial support and donations came in. We never had to worry about money. Blankets, mats, food, all of it was had for the asking. I snooped around and found the county warehouse where supplies are stored. I found a cache of blankets—hundreds of all-wool blankets stored in cases on the top of a shelf. "Hey, can I have some of those?" They gave me a hundred. A blanket to a homeless person is as good as gold. You don't want to turn it in every day, especially if you are caught out at night after the shelter has closed and it's cold outside and raining. There were times when a pitiful soul would knock at the door after midnight in a torrential rainstorm and because we had absolutely no room would be denied admittance. "Can you at least spare a blanket?", he would ask. I asked for another hundred. Well, this time they had to check. Request denied. Why? "These blankets are part of the emergency preparedness program specified by the Federal and State

Governments for every County." "What does that mean?" "They must be kept on hand in the event of a nuclear attack." I didn't even ask if they were kidding. I knew they weren't kidding.

Trying to get anything out of the bureaucracy was a revolving door. This only had to happen a few times—you go in here and you come out there, with nothing—the energy to undergo the process, after so many disappointments, is dissipated in advance.

We were told by the welfare representative that everyone in the shelter was potentially eligible for $120 a month, and, moreover, we could charge $180 a month rent and get that in addition. It turned out that because we were a "temporary shelter" we did not qualify as a permanent residence and therefore, unless an exception was made by the head bureaucrat, in each instance, our guests were not eligible.

One evening a homeless guy blew into the shelter with a letter from his lawyer boasting that he was the first person in the county without a permanent residence to beat the system and get a general assistance check. He had to sue to do it. His address was a local tree.

A word needs to be said about the homeless male and homeless female. There is welfare money immediately available for families and for women with children. But not for single people. I would not learn this lesson until I pursued the policies of the welfare system and that would take me five years. "Ve get so soon old und yet so late schmart", was a saying they had on the wall in Herbel's Meat Market across the street from where I lived in Milwaukee, Wisconsin. It was a piece of wisdom I picked up in my youth—it takes a long time to figure something out as complicated as the homeless problem and the welfare bureaucracy.

The homeless male constitutes the overwhelming majority in our programs. They were the ones who had no advocate when we began. A substantial group within that population was the homeless Vietnam veteran. No one even wanted to go near them. They were the victims of the Vietnam War. They would rather live in the woods than be the recipients of the charity of the local welfare system. Wouldn't you? It was a measure of their self-respect, as shattered as it was by what they had witnessed in Vietnam: they didn't want to be managed cases of the welfare system.

Beyond the Vietnam vets were all the other single adult males who had nowhere to go, nowhere to sleep, nowhere to eat, and nothing to do. They were unnecessary. They had disappeared. They were no accounts.

Peter Marin has written on the plight of the single adult male in *The Nation:*

> *"Often this goes unadmitted. Even when in deep trouble men understand, sometimes unconsciously, that they are not to complain or ask for help. I remember several men I knew in the local hobo jungle. Most of them were vets. They had constructed a tiny village of half-caves and shelters among the trees and brush, and when stove smoke filled the clearing and they stood bare to the waist, knives at their hips, you would swear you were in an army jungle camp. They drank throughout the day, and at dusk there always came a moment when they wandered off   individually to sit staring out at the mountains or sea. And you could see on their faces at such moments, if you caught them unawares, a particular and unforgettable look: pensive, troubled, somehow innocent—the look of lost children or abandoned men.*
>
> *"I have seen the same look multiplied hundreds of times on winter nights in huge shelters in great cities, where a thousand men at a time will sometimes gather, each encapsulated in solitude on a bare cot, coughing and turning or sometimes crying all night, lost in nightmares as terrible as a child's or as life on the street. In the mornings they returned to their masked public personas, to the styles of behavior and appearance that often frightened passers-by. But while they slept you could see past all that, and you found yourself thinking: These are still,*

even grown, somebody's children, and many fare no bet-
ter on their own, as adults, than they would have as chil-
dren."

It was principally the homeless adult male that we served at the Cedar Street Shelter and in the Interfaith Satellite Shelter.

Eventually, we had to move. Our lease was up and the owner had plans for remodeling the premises. We had to look for another site. Page organized a Site-selection Committee, which included some of the local personages, Mayor Mike Rotkin, and the head of the Chamber of Commerce, Lionel Stoloff. We looked around and found an excellent facility with lots of space. The landlord was cooperative although he knew it was going to be a hard sell for the other businesses in the building and adjoining. Things seemed to be going okay until the guy across the street—Leland Zeidler— who owned the Sashmill Complex, got wind of the deal and bought the building out from under us in order to scotch it. Just like that. We had to look elsewhere.

Eloise Smith directed us to an empty building on the corner of River Street (Highway 9) and Highway 1, which the University of California owned and, it turned out, wanted to sell. We jumped on it. The University, of course, wanted full market value. No concessions to the bleeding hearts in town. We had to raise part of the cost as an example of good faith, or I don't know what. A blood tax. A person who wished to remain anonymous sent in $30,000. In the meantime, we had started another program.

Chapter Three
The Interim: The Interfaith Satellite Shelter Program

Harassed by the authorities about occupancy restrictions, we figured something had to be done about the overflow while we were operating the Cedar Street Shelter. We were not in the business of turning homeless people away at the door during storms. The Rev. Paul Pfotenhauer, an old friend, and a local Lutheran minister, was a member of the Shelter Board, a group of concerned citizens and homeless providers who met to discuss the homeless problem. I asked him if he might take a group in at his church—Mount Calvary Lutheran—one night a week, just to make it easy on him. We would provide mats and blankets and transportation. He had a supportive congregation so he was a good one to ask. He checked and said yes they would do it. They were even willing to provide a hot meal for the group. The congregation took it as a great morale builder. We started appealing to other churches to fill out the week. Soon we had seven, one for every night of the week, all providing hot meals. We noticed that the morale of each congregation was significantly increased, with members of the congregation eager and willing to help. Page Smith took it to mean that the homeless were given by God to bring the churches of the land out of their bourgeois blues. He was right.

Nevertheless, it was a hard sell. On our part, there was no one else to turn to—no one in the City Government offered anything. The County was no better. The Churches were our only hope. The weather was a compelling arguing point. Unfortunately, it worked both ways. When the weather got better, the homeless were expected to fend for themselves. But when it was cold and wet, well, maybe... After we managed to organize seven churches, to cover the week, we eventually expanded to over forty churches, county-wide.

At the beginning, there was an unspoken directive: sneak them in and sneak them out. As long as they were invisible, (remember the theme?), it might work. We needed drivers to transport them to the churches. Fred Gray and I were the drivers. Fred drove people in his 1941 Chevy. It burned a rod bearing one night while he was transporting six guests to a church, but they eventually got there. Our pickup site was in front of the Civic Auditorium until the custodian complained. Then we moved over to the Louden Nelson Community Center.

Fred Gray was the Chair of the local FEMA Emergency Food and Shelter Board; he arranged for a $5,000 grant so we could buy a van, and for the delivery of 200 wool U.S. Army blankets. Fred was also the firm but gentle director of the interfaith program for the first three years, and continued the system by which homeless guests were responsible for the actual running of the program. Very radical stuff at the time. Eventually, we were able to collect enough blankets and buy enough mats so everyone had a minimally comfortable sleeping arrangement.

Thus was born the Interfaith Satellite Shelter Program (ISSP). Now with over forty participating churches, the budget has climbed from less than thirty thousand dollars to nearly two hundred thousand a year. In the last three years, the program has successfully competed for Federal Emergency Shelter Grant funding totalling four hundred and twenty thousand dollars. We provide a meal and shelter to as many as 150 people a night both in North and South County, between November and May, half of all homeless given shelter in the county. In the summer months, we drop down to thirty a night, in order to keep the program going year round. We plan to expand the program in 1992, to provide for sixty people each night, county-wide, during the summer months. We have a full time director, Andrew Morin, and two client service managers. We pay a corps of monitors to oversee the group, our largest budget item, recruited from the ranks of the homeless, who make the program work at the many shelter sites spread throughout the County.

Because of the program's simplicity and the crucial participation of local churches and their congregations and other individuals who volunteer their assistance, the Interfaith Satellite Shelter Program is one of the most cost-effective shelter programs for the homeless in California.

It was an interesting experience to watch this program develop. After we sneaked them in and sneaked them out on the premise that the lower the profile the better—nervous Nellies and nervous Nelsons in the congregation might complain—the churches began to accept them. We understood the reluctance. After all, it is hard enough going shopping on Pacific Ave., what with the homeless and the panhandlers and all, let alone having them sleeping in one's own church. And what about you know what (lice)? We passed all these hurdles when the word got out that we actually left the churches cleaner than we found them, although the custodians didn't appreciate that accolade. But it was a good line. Soon, we had tight little coteries of homeless sympathisers in every congregation in the group, providing meals, ministering, giving of themselves, learning names, and developing friendships.

We stored the mats and blankets for the program in my parents' garage next door to my home. The monitors started hanging around in my office (in my garage) where I was running the Platonic Academy, a nonprofit corporation devoted to my career in the herbal industry. I was trying to become computer competent at the time on an IBM clone and not having much luck. I don't take well to commands. It was before the Mac and the mouse, which I now use with perfect efficiency. One of the monitors was a computer whiz, so he started doing text entry for me. One day he told me about his involvement with cryptography while he was in the army. I said: "You know how to decipher? Look under your chair."

He pulled out my Voynich Manuscript box. He did nothing else for the next four months. He hardly looked up. He slept at my desk in my office and I had to bring him food. He had found the world's most mysterious manuscript, an herbal text written in a cipher, or an artificial language, thought to be by Roger Bacon, or a forgery by John Dee, but probably written by an Elizabethan herbalist named Anthony Askham. Nobody knew for sure. I had been working on it for years with my pal, the famous mathematician, Ralph Abraham.

The Voynich is named after a bookseller, a Mr. Voynich, who found the text in a trunk in an Italian monastery at the beginning of this century. This single copy is at the Beineke Library at Yale University where it is called the world's "most mysterious manuscript". I had been introduced to the Voynich by Dr. Leonell Strong, a famous geneticist, who claimed to have deciphered it and who thought it was by Anthony Askham, an Elizabethan herbalist. Dr. Strong died before carrying through his work, which I inherited. All of his notes and cipher workings were in the box under the chair the homeless guy was sitting on. I thought, as I watched him peruse the contents with mounting excitement: "will wonders never cease, God does work in mysterious ways. Here is a poor homeless guy who thinks he is going to crack the cipher of the world's most mysterious manuscript". He seemed equal to the task of carrying through the work of Dr. Strong. He was indefatigable.

After some months of intensive study, he was convinced Dr. Strong had successfully deciphered it. He thought he understood it. He was going to figure it all out. I supported him as best I could until he had a psychotic alcoholic breakdown and threatened to kill a university student we had recruited to help with the Old English part of the work. He finally left town with most of my material. I talk to him on the phone a couple times a year. His ex-girlfriend had seized all of his material, my material, and wouldn't give it up. In Phoenix, Arizona. One of those stories. So much for the world's most mysterious manuscript and the anticipated formula for the Elixir of Life which the manuscript presumably conceals.

But wait, hold the phone, he called last week and said the material was on the way, by mail, heavily insured. Maybe, after long last.... I'll believe it when I see it.

Another monitor who looked a little like a very skinny pit bull lurked around outside my parents' garage once in a while after we no longer stored the mats and blankets there. What the hell was he doing in the driveway at 8:00 am when I went out to get the newspaper? He always had on a fancy racing bike outfit which took me off guard. When I asked him what he wanted, it always turned out to be $30.00 I gave it to him. I didn't know he was a cocaine addict and a thief. He wound up stealing a suitcase full of paper I brought back from an herbal trip to China. The mailman returned it after he found it two blocks away in a field. He stole a little motorbike that didn't work and left it a block and a half away when he couldn't start it. I noticed it and brought it back home. He stole a new briefcase I had bought in Hong Kong where I kept a precious manuscript I had written when I turned fifty and had a short fit of inspiration: *The Long Lost Last Dialogues of Socrates.*

I had done a psychic dig on the site of the Platonic Academy (my garage— oh, come on, this is Santa Cruz) and had come up with some dialogues that Socrates had taken part in after he had been presumedly executed. His friends, instead of the notorious hemlock, had administered an herbal concoction that induced a deep trance state and simulated death, so his body was given over to his friends for burial. He survived, unbeknownst to the authorities, revived, and was kept in hiding for three years before he died from natural causes. This is what he said during those three years. The secret dialogues of Socrates. It was terrific, I thought, me, writing like Plato and talking like Socrates. I even appended to the title page an old antique post card I had received from a former student showing the prison where Socrates had been kept, in the side of a hill, outside of Athens.

It was my only copy. When I confronted him after the theft, he said he had put the briefcase on a driveway a block away after he found out it contained nothing of worth to him. It was not returned.

Oh well, that's another price I've had to pay. I was very attached to that manuscript; I don't care what the Buddhists say.

We had an annual Thanksgiving Dinner for the homeless at the Presbyterian Church on Mission and Highland, with turkeys galore. We found that when you learn someone's name, they are no longer 'homeless'; they are a person; they have not disappeared, or, if they have, they reappear, just like that; they are Tom or Jean or Bill or Charlotte. It was as simple as that: common human decency at work. Both ways. And when you sat down to a meal with them, then they were as good as family.

I had second thoughts about that at the Thanksgiving Dinner in 1989. I did a double take. There he was. He had been a figure on the campus, at UCSC, when I was teaching there over two decades ago. He must have been released from prison, because there he was, helping himself to turkey. I turned to my wife and raised my eyebrows and pointed him out to her. Once he had come to our house and stood at the front door, in a kind of trance, I guess, nose to the door. My wife happened to open the door and there he was. She screamed and slammed the door in his face He was enough to scare anyone. It is a wonder that someone like that can be tolerated as long as he is. He first showed up in my Bible Class, which I happened to be teaching at the time as the Chairman of Religious Studies. He was my reward for having the lack of temerity to teach the Bible at a state university. He raised his hand at the opening of the first class and he said: "If you have any trouble with any interpretation, don't hesitate; as I'm God, feel free to call on me. I'll be happy to contribute." Everyone in the class winced with me.

He was very tall and he was dressed in a white floor-length robe. His hair was peroxided yellow. There was an aroma of sulphur about him. He looked like he had stepped out of a *New Yorker* cartoon.

One day he came to my office. "It is unseemly for God to go without", he said, a great opening line. "I am appointing you as my Faculty Tithing Chairman and you and your colleagues will give 10% of your salary to support me and my work, which you, as Chairman, will collect."

It's the only time during my entire teaching career I remember getting pissed off at anyone in my office in terms of losing my temper; I mean I turned black. I felt this black fluid start at my feet and come up my legs and when it hit my head, I said in a tone so ominous, I frightened myself: "Get out of here. Get out!" He left.

Months later, he kicked an Afro-American to death in the parking lot of the Holiday Inn, in downtown Santa Cruz. The man had played Jesus in an off-beat local play: "Tuna Christ." "God" didn't like that. He went to jail. Now, twenty years later, he was back, sitting at our homeless Thanksgiving dinner, helping himself to a drumstick, looking absolutely batty.

The homeless mentally ill represent up to fifty percent of the homeless population. This guy was an exception to the rule, as most of the so-called mentally ill are simply eccentric and no harm to themselves or others, even though they are in desperate need of counseling and support. The lack of mental health resources is one of the most serious problems facing homeless service providers and is at the root of why many of the homeless are unable to break out of the homeless cycle. We see young men in reasonable physical shape adrift on the streets abandoned to their own lack of resources in the spiral of despair and defeat with no one to turn to for help and support.

The most evident impression of the homeless participating in the Church Satellite Program was how *subdued* they were, Thanksgiving or not, when they arrived at the churches. They just wanted to turn in after the meal. They were tired. Some were exhausted. No one wanted trouble. They just wanted to lie down and get some sleep out of harm's way. They wanted rest from their conflicts.

The support of the churches and the local synagogue gave us the basis for the work we had to do. They were our foundation. Without them, it would have been very difficult; with them, we had a coalition of a broad spectrum of Protestant, Roman Catholic, and Jewish support. It gave our efforts a credibility and a base in the community that was unassailable. They all knew what the Bible said about the homeless, the poor, the afflicted, the needy, the downtrodden. Shiloh Superfly was right. His prophetic passages were being fulfilled in our midst.

At the end of our fifth year of operation—June, 1991—our statistics were quite stunning—22,423 people had been given shelter over the year, up 64% from the previous year and 179% from the year before, basically the same one hundred every night, with some fluctuations in the group. The increased numbers were partly due to the expansion of the program into Watsonville. The North County Program expanded from 80 beds a night to 112, and from 15 beds a night during the summer season to 30. Because the demand lessens when the weather improves, we reduce the service from May to November. This is also due to budgetary considerations.

The County of Santa Cruz has contributed no funds to the Interfaith Satellite Program for the coming fiscal year (1991-2) knowing that the Federal grants do not provide for administration; why, I don't know. It is a kind of Catch-22. If you don't have the money to run the program, we won't give you money for the program. Or, conversely, we'll give you money for the program but you have to find the money to run it. However, the County does help administer the Federal funds that support the program and that has been generously supplied.

Perusing the County Budget is my favorite toilet time reading. You get the impression that those in charge don't even read it on any occasion. Why all the chairs, why all the desks, why all the computers, why the love seat at Juvenile Hall (for over $1,000), why so much of it, the heart grows weary and sick over every page. And then they have the gall to tell you there is no money for the homeless. The waste, the pork barrel, the padding, the fraud is *prima facie*—it is there staring you in the face. Years ago, we helped the Community Congress get started out of our William James Association offices. They red penciled the County Budget wherever they thought unnecessary expenses were being entered for a new carpet, a new set of office furniture, additional elevators, for god's sake, let them walk up the stairs, all the perks of the bureaucrats. Millions of dollars were transferred to human services. We have to do it again. No one can tell me out of a budget of a quarter billion dollars, the amount of money the County spends every year, hardly a dime can be spared for the homeless. I would like to make the supervisor who told me there was no money for the homeless eat the budget and watch him do it in public. Werner Herzog* would be invited to film it.

By comparison, the River Street Shelter, which the Citizens Committee for the Homeless no longer administers, serving one-third the population of the Interfaith Satellite Shelter, has a budget of $250,000 and receives almost $200,000 in funding from the County. The River Street Shelter is administered by the Santa Cruz Community Counseling Center. It is an example of favored status in terms of a highly organized and staffed non-profit wired to the County and budgetary considerations.

*Werner Herzog Eats His Shoe is a film by Les Blanc.

30

There is no public scrutiny of budgets by people competent to review them outside of the bureaucratic and administrative agencies involved, no rational planning, and no long-range goals. The newly formed Homeless Action Network involving many of the providers of homeless services may evolve into performing this needed function. As it stands, programs simply grow of their own dynamic and secure whatever funds are available without coordination with other programs and services and without sharing resources

Interfaith Satellite Shelter Program

Over the last three years the Interfaith Satellite Shelter (ISSP) has responded to the growing plight of the homeless by expanding its shelter services to become the largest homeless shelter program in Santa Cruz County. Three years ago during the program year 1988-89, ISSP provided 8,050 Person Shelter Days (PSDs). For 1991-92, ISSP is expected to provide approximately 27,000 PSDs, an increase of 235%. ISSP has increased participation of local churches in the program from twenty one churches in 1988-89, to thirty eight churches in 1991-92. At the same time the budget for ISSP has grown from about $50,000 in 1988-89, to almost $200,000 in 1991-92. However, the budget for ISSP remains a fraction of other homeless shelter programs, including programs that are considerably smaller than ISSP. ISSP provides shelter and a meal for one person for about $7.25, making the program one of the most cost effective inthe State of California. The savings that ISSP achieves in providing its shelter services are due to the volunteer participation of Santa Cruz County churches and their congregations, and also the participation of other local citizens who volunteer their time and money to provide meals at ISSP shelter sites.

ISSP Budget 1991-92 (Est.) $196,000

Participating Churches in the Interfaith Satellite Shelter Program.

All Saints' Episcopal *Watsonville*
Aptos Community Methodist Church *Aptos*
Arthur Road Baptist *Watsonville*
Boulder Creek Methodist Women
   Boulder Creek
Calvary Chapel *Santa Cruz*
Calvary Episcopal Church *Santa Cruz*
Christ Lutheran *Aptos*
Church of Christ Scientist *Santa Cruz*
Community Covenant *Scotts Valley*
Community Covenant Church *Scotts Valley*
Community Lutheran *Watsonville*
First Baptist *Capitola*
First Baptist *Watsonville*
First Baptist Church *Santa Cruz*
First Congregational *Santa Cruz*
First Congregational *Soquel*
First Presbyterian Church *Santa Cruz*
First United Methodist *Watsonville*
Garfield Park Christian Church *Santa Cruz*
Good Shepherd School *Santa Cruz*
Grace United Methodist Church
   Santa Cruz
Holy Eucharist Catholic *Watsonville*
La Selva Community *La Selva Beach*

Light House Christian Fellowship *Soquel*
Light of Life Lutheran Church *Scotts Valley*
Live Oak Methodist *Live Oak*
Messiah Lutheran (*Santa Cruz*)
Mt. Calvary Lutheran (*Soquel*)
National Guard Armory
National Guard Armory (*Freedom*)
Reorganized Church of Latter Day Saints
Resurrection Catholic Church *Aptos*
Salvation Army *Watsonville*
San Augustin Church *Scotts Valley*
Santa Cruz Friends Meeting *Santa Cruz*
Santa Cruz Missionary Baptist *Santa Cruz*
Seventh Day Adventist *Watsonville*
Seventh Day Adventist Church *Santa Cruz*
St. Andrews Presbyterian *Aptos*
St. Patrick's Catholic *Watsonville*
St. Philips Episcopal *Scotts Valley*
St. Stephan's Lutheran *Santa Cruz*
Star of the Sea Catholic *Santa Cruz*
Temple Bethel *Soquel*
Trinity Presbyterian Church *Santa Cruz*
Unitarian Univeralist Fellowship *Aptos*
United Presbyterian *Watsonville*
Unity Temple *Soquel*

On March 5th, 1992, Paul Pfotenhauer and I went over to Monterey to speak to a group of ministers and homeless advocates to encourage them to start a program similar to ours. We had been over a couple times before but the timing wasn't right and nothing came of it. This time six churches signed up and we were dutifully gratified. County Supervisor Sam Karas was in attendance and pledged his support for the venture. If they hurry, they can write a grant in the two weeks left to them and apply for money from the same Federal funds that support our program in Santa Cruz.

I'm a little tired of hearing about these people as if they're ready for sainthood.

Santa Cruz Chief of Police, Bassett, commenting on the homeless, as reported in the national press.

Chapter Four
The River Street Shelter and the Counter-Advocate Reaction

Eventually we were able to obtain the River Street Shelter as a permanent shelter site on a purchase from the University. The deal almost fell through a number of times and but for a spontaneous trip to Berkeley by Page Smith, to encounter the minor bureaucrat in charge of negotiations, we would have lost out on the deal. After Page presented himself in the guy's office (and in his face) and made known his concern, the guy finally said we could ask for an extension of the bargaining time, a small point he had neglected to tell us until then, after we thought our time had run out.

There are always little loopholes all around the block for you to find out about, if you're lucky, or, better yet, experienced in the ways of the world. The "worldliness of the world", a very negative biblical term, has come to fulfillment in the triumph of the obtuse bureaucrats—those who man the so-called infrastructures of our institutions. They play games with you, sometimes semantic. "If you can't waive the fee" (it would set a *precedent*, a bad word to a bureaucrat), "how about indefinitely postponing it?" "Oh, that we can do."

You have to have a consultant to learn how to talk to an obtuse bureaucrat. Another needless expense.

One could have kept a log of such examples, so many are they, to indict the dunderheads who get in the way, but what's the point? It's all part of the process. Better develop a thick skin than take it personally. Better the woods than the trees. "Perserverance furthers", as the *I Ching* says. Keep your eye on the prize. Institutional process over idiosyncratic display. I learned that working with Alan Chadwick and the UCSC Garden

Project in our negotiations with the university, my first learning experience in terms of encountering the triumph of the obtuse bureaucrat, the spectre haunting higher education in California.

When the River Street Shelter opened, certain officials took credit for it where little or no credit was due. They appeared at the formal opening, which they, of course, had organized and we didn't even attend. Our shelter. A few of us lurked outside wondering where these guys got off congratulating themselves on being obstacles we had overcome. But it was at least the beginning of some small support from the County and the City that would eventually build into a fairly solid program on presumably very scant resources. This is my small concession, by way of a clumsy sentence, to working with the powers that be.

Fred Gray, who had appeared in the opening days of the Cedar Street Shelter, advised us on County/City conflicts, where we got caught in the crossfire without quite knowing why anyone was shooting. We were uninformed about the history of the conflicts between the City and the County and he explained why things were so complicated and why we were a pawn on the chess board. He helped us get some operating money for the running of the shelter. He was the Executive Director of the Community Action Board (CAB) at the time and knew his way around the infrastructures. He became the first Director of the River Street Shelter and also helped organize and run the Interfaith Satellite Shelter. He was perfectly qualified for the job and knew exactly how to handle an extremely difficult situation of which organizing and operating a shelter for the homeless was a prime example.

In order to obtain and operate the River Street Shelter, Fred Gray proposed that the City buy the property and the County provide operating money. Purchase price was $539,000, or the assessed value. Operating money for the first year was $110,000. Fred had identified the money for the purchase in the City accounts before asking for it, which should be highlighted as a very smart procedure. They can't say no if you know they have the money sitting there with no concrete plans to use it. Fred also used his inside knowledge of City affairs to ferret out the fact that the City's bid to the university was consciously set a full $100,000 below the minimum bid, which we knew would be unacceptable. Armed with this knowledge, which was tightly held within the City offices, we were able to announce a fundraising drive of $100,000 just prior to the City submitting it's bid. This effectively locked in the deal. It was very unlikely that the City would then back out of the deal. Our clear understanding was that the City had intended that the bid would be rejected, leaving the university as the bad guy.

As of November 1987, we had a centralized emergency shelter on a permanent basis and a well-organized Interfaith Satellite Shelter Program to accomodate the overflow. Our goal was never to turn anyone away who was looking for a place to sleep. All we had to do was add another church. Fortunately, there were churches to spare.

In an unused garage attached to the shelter so much donated clothing spontaneously appeared that a free used clothing center was spawned. Volunteers appeared who sorted and organized the mass of clothing and this effort in itself developed as a major project. Sandy Loranger was an amazingly dedicated and organized person who turned the mounds of clothing into an organized shop, complete with sized and labled articles of clothing. It was a kick to see a local street figure named Shadow sitting at a sewing machine and mending clothes.

The level of interest on the part of County officials, as evidenced by a notorious memo on official stationary, concerned itself with newspapers blowing around the driveway and why drapes didn't match (the furniture was donated). It was predictable that those public officials who were so interested in the physical facility, rarely showed any real interest in the true work of the shelter— the guests. We did get donated metal frame beds from the City Property Manager, Lisa Rose, and mattresses from the university, and were thus able to furnish the shelter with almost no expense.

Television sets, answering machines, food, kitchen utensils, linens, toys, magazines and books, landscaping supplies, all came in through the front door as though by magic. We never turned anything away even though we wound up with a large accumulation of odds and ends. But it revealed to us again that the resources for supplying such an enterprise seemed inexhaustible, whereas bureaucratized institutional sets discourage and hardly respond to such donations.

Fred had a kind of personal radar system and seemed to know about homeless people who were not sheltered because they were so indigent and out of it they were lost to their own devices. He located a 72 year old man in a rainsoaked sleeping bag in a business suit, where, for five days, he had been waiting the return of a friend who had gone off to cash the old man's social security check. He was crippled and unable to move and he would have died as his friend was not going to return. He was brought to the shelter and cared for. Adult Protective Services had closed his file thinking he had died. It is not an easy fate to end up under the conservatorship of a county agency.

It was not the first time that we registered the unfortunate conflict between case-management and non-institutionalized person-to-person concern and care. Although the professional social service care is based on case-management, the model of social welfare systems in this country, it is important to allow for non-professional concern and programs such as our own, where the word 'case' is never used. The fact that social services do not work well under public institutions, and that public social service institutions do not tolerate private efforts they can't control is a clear lesson of this experience.

During the twenty months we operated the River Street Shelter, there was only one fight. That fist-fight was not between clients but between two staff people. It is unfortunate that the basis for the brawl was racism; still, it seems remarkable that this was the worst of it, given the level of disturbance and crisis that many clients were burdened with. I can only credit the remarkable record of peaceful process to Fred Gray's humane and caring attitude, which supported an environment of trust and mutual respect.

A major source of operating funds for the River Street Shelter came from County Mental Health Services. The lack of available rental space and emergency shelter space for the emotionally and mentally disabled clients of Mental Health made the deal attractive for the County. The River Street Shelter became the place where County Mental Health put its most difficult "cases". The level of trust and acknowledgement that this implied in our ability to be productive and supportive of people in grave crisis unfortunately didn't carry over to vocal support.

We suffered from the fact that our administrative support unit, under the non-profit with which we were then affiliated, was understaffed and over-burdened. This left Fred and his staff with the bulk of the administrative work as well as the direct work with clients. This was quite a burden. It was remarkable the degree to which they were able to be productive with the clients and maintain the burden of the administrative work.

Almost as soon as we were up and operating, Page Smith started voicing his idea for Community House, a permanent rental/shelter to be built on the vacant lot behind the River Street Shelter. This would provide a room for the homeless who would always be in need of an inexpensive place to stay either because of some disability or because they would nev-er make enough money to afford local rents. But the main reason was stability. The River Street Shelter, like most shelters, was transient. You could only stay a month and then you had to move on. Where? Wherever. We needed a facility that would afford a permanent room on a very low rental basis for those who qualified.

Fred ran the shelter for the nearly two years we operated it. During that time we had to cope with the counter-productive tactics of Robert Norse, a self-styled homeless advocate who suddenly appeared one day out of the blue. We had no idea where he came from and what he was up to except that he was going to be trouble, not only to the local authorities, but also to us. He reminded us of the worst vision of a 1960s "outside agitator" type who comes to town to fuss things up. The type that never does any-thing productive, and never means to do anything productive—but is especially good at making a fuss. For its own sake. An old style *agent provocateur* with a t-shirt reading *"epater le bourgeoisie"*. There were those among us, especially Fred, who came to believe that Robert intended to cause disruption for the benefit of those who wanted our enterprise to fail. Most of us came to believe that he lived off an annuity of some sort and was free to agitate full time. Moreover, he got lots of press.

Robert enlisted Jane Imler and she joined forces with him to attack our work. The main complaint was that we were spending too much money for the number of homeless we could accommodate. It wasn't our fault. We were stuck with the obtuse zoning rule that only so many people per toilet were allowed to stay at the shelter—a terrific condition for home-less housing—so we were tied up with adding additional toilet facilities in order to increase our capacity. We were allowed 16 people per day and even though there were 30 people on a bad night, we averaged 17 over a period of 20 months. This fact, that we were able to accommodate more people on nasty wet and cold nights, and still average only 17 people was not something which sat well with the public entities that floated above us. They wanted to know just *why* we had exceeded our quota of 16. It was the same old crap from Cedar Street all over again. Nit picking on the numbers on any given night.

The garage at the Shelter, which had operated so well as a free clothing shop was eventually remodeled by the City into dormitory units accommo-dating another 14 people and adding another two bathrooms. The City needed to give itself a use permit to allow the use of the remodeled garage. The dormitory units were thus left unused for two weeks during the winter. So Jane and friends staged a protest sit-in in one of the dormi-tory's bathtubs on New Year's Eve and were arrested for trespassing. I could hardly blame her even though the woman whose life we had saved by opening a shelter was attacking us. She failed to distinguish between us and the City and County. I started to think it would have been better to have let her starve to death and *then* opened a shelter. The complaints were mostly nit picking complaints, we thought, irritating and against the grain. But it depended on whose side you were on in this division within the homeless advocate groups.

Wait a minute. Weren't we in this together? Why attack your fellow advocates who were finally getting a decent program together? Well, it was a big fall out. Fred was on the line and we were caught in between. We weren't much help. It was a process we had to work through. Given enough time, Norse would completely discredit himself even in the eyes of the homeless, just those whom he meant to represent. They wanted to punch him out.

It was a bad period with a lot of bad publicity. We held our breath...and our noses. The worst moment in it all was when the Mayor at the time—Mardi Wormhoudt—a woman capable of phenomenally aggressive and ill-tempered vibes, whom I grew to dislike with a passion, called out the Attack Troops, also known as the SWAT Team, to harass the homeless protesting the camping ban.

Outside of our church program there was nowhere to get a meal at night. Jane Imler and friends made soup available at the Town Clock as the evening meal for the homeless. The Mayor didn't like that and took steps to stop it. It all looks ragged and rather silly now, but at the time, it made Santa Cruz look foolish and mendacious in the eyes of the nation as the incident was reported in the national media. The Mayor insisted you had to have a permit to give a hungry homeless person a sandwich and you had to have an inspected and certified kitchen to give someone homeless a cup of soup. Anything to get in the way of free food. It was a very bad episode.

And then Mitch Snyder came to town, for the second time. He had already come to Santa Cruz at Page Smith's invitation the previous summer, but I was in Northern Wisconsin, so I missed him. The second time, I met him at the Town Clock, where he had come to show his solidarity with the protesters. He was very grim, very serious, very taciturn, and battle-worn, wearing a worn battle jacket. I gave him a bear hug as a comrade in arms. He wanted to know how we could bear to suffer under a city and a mayor that prevented giving food to the homeless. He cut through it all like a hot knife in butter. After all, he had brought Reagan to his knees, after fasting on him at the door of the White House, one irascible Irishman to another, and had finally been given his shelter, a campaign promise of Reagan, which he dragged his feet on after he was elected, one of the largest in the country, where he would eventually hang himself in his room.

It was a very black day when I got the news and had to accept the fact that despair and suicide had overcome one of our heroes. I had seen him again at the National March For the Homeless, in Washington, D.C., in October, of 1989, where a large contingent had gone from Santa Cruz. He was striding across the hillside of the Washington Monument, my favorite object in the whole world, where everyone gathered for the march. I took his picture. It was a day of triumph for him, given the nationwide outpouring of concern and sympathy for the cause of which he was the symbolic spokesman.

As the national spokesman for the homeless, you could see it in every pore of his personality, in the fibre of his being, in his tone of voice. In my youth, I had been deeply influenced by Dorothy Day and the Catholic Worker movement, all the way back to my Lutheran Seminary days, around 1954, in St. Paul, Minnesota. I was actually the agent for the Catholic Worker newspaper at Luther Theological Seminary, where I was a student. It has dutifully arrived in the mail ever since. I had even visited them in New York, at the Catholic Worker headquarters, where I met Ammon Hennacy, Dorothy Day's sidekick. He gave me an autographed copy of his autobiography: *Confessions of a Christian Anarchist*. I liked Christian anarchists. Snyder was in the same tradition. He was burning with the passion of his cause and everyone withered, by comparison, before his gaze.

Recently, I saw Martin Sheen on a television interview program talking about his friendship with Mitch and how, when he went to Washington to spend some time with him, Mitch asked him how many pairs of shoes he had. "Two", said Sheen, in terms of what he had in his suitcase. "Well, you only need one pair. Give your other pair to someone who has none."

He was like that. He reminded me of a title of one of Kierkegaard's *Edifying Discourses:* "The Purity of Heart Is To Will One Thing."

Then came the right-wing backlash against the homeless radicals— Carolyn Busenhart and company— the "Take Back Our Town" people, a no more absurd slogan for narrow and mean-spirited minds. They wore red shirts out of some color blind affinity with Brown Shirts, apparently to go with their red necks. An ugly lot. I thought someone on our side had paid her and her ilk to act out the worst side of the opposition in order to generate more sympathy for our cause. In any event, that was the consequence of her organized protest.

Robert Norse had called for the homeless to gather in Santa Cruz over the 4th of July holiday. So the Red Shirts stood on the sidewalk and cursed and spit and acted stupid as the homeless walked by. They had an even briefer shelf life than Norse.

All the heat died down, and a compromise was reached to serve food on the site of the River Street Shelter, an obvious solution. After all, there were those who declined to use the Interfaith Satellite Shelter Program, where they could get an evening meal. They didn't want to go to a church where they could sleep on the floor. What about them? Maybe as many as fifty up to one hundred or more. Before she left town, Jane Imler and Paddy Long organized the effort to feed this neglected group, much to their credit, and with the help of the homeless, they began serving a hot meal every late afternoon. She called it "Calamity's Cupboard", as in "Calamity Jane" and we made her operation an affiliate of the William James Association, to give her the auspices of a nonprofit corporation.

One thing led to another and what with Jane's poor health, Karen Gillette, who was employed by the County Human Resources Agency, took over the effort after Jane dropped out with Paddy Long continuing to help on a daily basis.

Chapter Five
The Free Meal Program

Operated by the homeless themselves, A Free Meal is overseen by Karen Gillette, as volunteer coordinator. She succeeded Jane Imler in the effort to offer a free meal to the homeless every afternoon. It was also a reaction to the antics of Robert Norse coming from the homeless themselves. They began to realize that the fighting going on (presumably in their behalf) was never going to lead anywhere and seemed to be fomented for its own sake. They were tired of it. They were tired of the politics, tired of watching the homeless walk all over town in search of the "political stew", a moveable feast if there ever was one. The County had offered a kitchen and this offer was accepted by the new group.

Brian Koepke named it "A Free Meal", in part, meaning free from Robert Norse. He became *persona non grata* at the site. They were tired of his confrontational mode of politics in their behalf. Instead, the homeless turned a cooperative face to the authorities, willing to work in common toward a common goal. The confrontational episode was over.

Even the "post office table" and those who manned it, decided to fold up their very public image, which took lots of flack, and go over and volunteer to help serve at The Free Meal. They brought a kind of anarchistic independence with them, working as hard as they had fought in terms of their very public presence outside the Santa Cruz Post Office. The Free Meal became known for its militant self-help spirit, in large part because of this group of volunteers.

The atmosphere of the site is not that of a soup kitchen where most people are dour and depressed. It has more of the atmosphere of a college dorm or a Grateful Dead parking lot scene without the concert. A common question asked by a visitor is: why is everyone so cheerful here?

The enthusiasm is tangible.

Underneath and supporting the festive mood is a serious commitment. A Free Meal is a world within a world, where everyone feels equal, everyone feels respected, and everyone feels valued. It is a living example of how our society should work, freely, with no ulterior motives and no hidden agendas. Those who can work take care of those who cannot work and without passing judgement.

Up to two hundred people are served on a given evening. Over the past year (1990-91), A Free Meal has continued to provide a safe gathering place for shelterless Santa Cruz residents, serving over 72,000 meals. The mealsite has become the focal point of the homeless community, providing a much-needed sense of place for those who would otherwise have none and no where to go for an evening meal.

The level of volunteer support is extremely high, allowing costs to be kept at a minimum. At this point, the potential of their self-help group has exceeded the size of the program. They have many more job applicants than positions, and more volunteers than actual work to be done. It is this combination of enthusiasm and hard work that drives A Free Meal. The Homeless Community Resource Center, to be organized along the same lines as A Free Meal, will be organized with the same spirit and will involve the homeless in the organization and administration of the program.

The other afternoon I paid a visit to the Free Meal in order to get a first hand impression of the operation and to get some names.

The cooks are Mike Hobson and Roger Westlock. The Field Manager is Mike Carltock. From my perspective, he is one of the reasons for the good vibes. He buys the food and sees to the problem of keeping order. The food is largely obtained from the Food Bank where foodstuffs are sold at .14 cents a pound whether it is rice or beans or cheese or vegetables,, butter, bread, tea, coffee, dried milk, sugar, *etc.*. It is due to this inexpensive source that the cost of a meal is about 45 cents a person. The program runs on about $500 a week. The meal served that day was pasta, pretty much standard fare, call it lasagna another day, moving on to soup, rice and whatever. Robin Hernandez is the dishwasher and Rose Santana is a dishwasher and baker. Our old friend Paddy Long invariably shows up and helps out making mental notes on what to look for at the Flea Market in terms of tools and supplies, striking up conversations and sustaining friendships. Community service workers on court referral and volunteers fill out the work force. The number one problem, I was told, was alcohol, which usually meant fights and unruly behaviour. The chronic boozers were well known and fairly well contained. Peer pressure works like a charm when you think your program is in jeopardy so everyone pitches in to keep the boat from being rocked. There were only two rules: no drunks or no alcohol on the premises and no fighting. Although the program is in a current financial crunch, it is assumed that funds will be found to continue serving meals. It is too important a program to allow to lapse.

If anything proves my idea of entropynerds into entrepreneurs it is the Interfaith Satellite Monitors, the Free Meal staff and volunteers, the Homeless Gardeners, and the Service Center—to be organized with this principle in mind, where the homeless are given the chance to consider the projects as their own rather than imposed upon them. Then all of the untapped and unutilised energy has the opportunity to show itself.

Chapter Six
Community House

As we have already described it, if you don't mind a little review, our efforts in behalf of the homeless began in December of 1985, when the William James Association, of which Page Smith and I are the Co-Directors, undertook to run a shelter for single males and some women, on Cedar Street, in downtown Santa Cruz. When the lease, taken out by the County, without discussion with the City, expired, in March, the Santa Cruz Citizens Committee for the Homeless, a newly formed non-profit superseding the William James Association, looked for a new site.

After an extensive search the property at River Street was located and chosen by the site selection committee consisting of several members of the City Council and representatives of the business community (Downtown Association and Chamber of Commerce). The University of California was preparing to sell the property which it had purchased from the State in 1964 for overflow housing for students. As stated, the property was appraised at something in the neighborhood of $539,000.

The Santa Cruz Citizens Committee for the Homeless raised approximately $100,000 toward the purchase price. It was this money which gave dramatic evidence of community support for the venture and made the whole deal possible.

The deed of sale specified that the property could only be used for beneficial public purposes but the land had hardly been acquired before the City Council, lead by Mayor Wormhoudt, began trying to sell the portion of property not in active use as a shelter, somewhat less than an acre, for commercial purposes. They thought they could sneak this through behind the back of the Citizens Committee. These efforts were tireless and covert. We can only assume that the purpose was to be able to refute the public charge that the City Council had recklessly expended public funds to purchase a property used by only 35 homeless or about $20,000 per bed, even though the money came from federal sources.

Unable to overcome our opposition, the City was persuaded to sell the property to the Citizens Committee even though it had already been purchased for the homeless. Get it? We had to buy the land we had already arranged to be bought for the homeless one more time, as though to penalize our efforts. The City had the less- than-an-acre appraised for $425,000. The City then said it would sell us that portion of the property, the whole of which we had worked so hard to help buy, for $350,000. We would have to find that amount of money to buy property we had already acquired for the homeless. The more we repeated this fact, the less it helped us to understand it.

The purpose of the purchase and what we had in mind ever since organizing the River Street Shelter was to build Community House for the long-term homeless—elderly homeless and those with physical and mental disabilities, in other words, those in most need for a permanent room for the rest of their lives.

We agreed to raise the additional $350,000 and we did so. Paul Pfotenhauer and Fred Gray managed to raise $125,000 from two Lutheran groups, and Fred managed to secure $225,000 from the American Red Cross, in the wake of the earthquake. We applied to the Department of Housing and Community Development for a grant of $725,000, for the construction of Community House and we asked our friend, Mark Primack, a local architect, to design it.

On March lst, we found out that we did not receive the State funds, in the first round of the cycle. Two steps had been left out of the process, steps we were not informed about. We had to have a Public Hearing. Why? And we had to have a management plan. Why hadn't that been clear all along? We suspected sabotage originating from the local level. Then we found out that a number of other conditions would have to be met before the City would cooperate any further and close escrow.

Finally, on June 11, 1991, all the conditions were met and we closed escrow. We own the property already owned for the homeless. But, now, instead of it being city property, it belongs to the Citizens Committee for the Homeless. We had paid our blood tax.

In early July, we found out that we had been denied State funds on the third round of the submission of our grant request. Seemingly specious reasons were given for our denial. Our grant is under appeal as we prepare another application and look for other sources for funding.

When I returned from Wisconsin at the end of the summer of 1991, I eyeballed the property driving by on Highway 1 and there the tents were—an *ad hoc* campground was clearly evident from the freeway. I had heard about it by phone during the summer. Homeless people who had always camped there and had kept a very low profile sneaking in at night and sleeping under one of the large trees on the property were now pitching tents and slowly over time a campsite had developed. Some fifty people, it was estimated, were sleeping there at night. The police had been alerted to the situation and the very humane and understanding Assistant Chief of Police—Lt. Dunbaugh—was willing to cooperate with the situation as long as the campers were willing to police themselves and minimize difficulties. Drunks had been dealt with by forcing them to move off the property. They had taken up residence a block away.

I went down to take a look with Paul Pfotenhauer to see how things were going. After all, it was our property and we were responsible for what was happening there now that we had closed escrow and had acquired the site from the city. Everything seemed fine. Brian Koepke immediately stepped up to talk to us, an old friend and homeless advocate, himself homeless. He assured us that things were going smoothly now that the drunks were gone. The garbage was picked up. No fights. Just homeless people in pup tents sleeping in the field.

Then the local paper ran an article and it looked as though we would have to shut down the *ad hoc* campground. We were hoping to keep things going until the Interfaith Shelter opened on November 1st in terms of the expanded operation. We were only trying to buy three weeks of time.

We were not about to post the site and subject homeless people, our con-stituents, to be arrest, for trespassing. It is an example of double binds the social order forces upon you—arresting homeless people for camping on property designated for a homeless shelter.

Now tell me about use permits. Tell me about politicians who know full well what is going on and then, when the news gets out, cover their ass, as the saying goes, by denying all knowledge. Tell me about sticking it to the have-nots as a kind of American pastime spectator sport. We seem to have become a society that dwells on targeting the victim. It could be called "beating a dead horse."

The Board of the Citizens Committee met to deliberate on the issue. We decided we would not post the property. We would not order the home-less off. We would not abandon them to find some other out-of-the-way place, but, instead, would open a site within the Interfaith Satellite Shelter Program, a church with a campground, to accommodate those who would avail themselves of it.

The next night Page Smith slept out on the field and I went down to spend a couple of hours with him. It was Friday night. I made a tour of the field and could not locate him. He was indistinguishable from the other campers. A homeless woman whom I appealed to, took me over to him There he was next to the fence in his sleeping bag, one of America's greatest living historians, my pal, stretched out on the ground. The group around him was a little raucous, loud laughter, some high spirits, some music, but not too loud. We talked things over.

I was reminded of a visit from Donald and Dorothy Nicholl, two weeks before. Dorothy had told me about a national sleep-out in behalf of the homeless throughout Great Britain. She had slept out in some town square. Here was Page starting our own version all by himself.

The deadline for the *ad hoc* campground arrived on Monday evening and only Robert Norse and two followers, one drunk, were arrested. A portable toilet was torched later that night and it cost us $500. All of the campers who wanted to go were taken by van to the camping site next to

Mount Calvary Lutheran Church where those who had no tent were provided with one thanks to Paddy Long. We made arrangements for them to be picked up and brought back every day so they could get into town and avail themselves of the free meal. We considered it a successful solution to a difficult situation.

Some unnamed advocates on our side cooked up a small prank and took the torched toilet and deposited it on Robert Norse's front lawn, with a little graffiti added, addressed to him. It was a self-evident statement.

Amid all the furor over the use of the property, through those intervening months, Fred Gray, in the role of Project Director, Mark Primack, our Architect, and Thom McCue, from Housing For Independent People Inc., have managed to secure a Design and Special Use Permit from the City for Community House, and a $40,000 grant, contingent on approval of our request to the State for $630, 000 of construction money. Many issues of concern had to be addressed before the City could sign off on our design. Our team was able to provide the right answers to the City's questions.

We have submitted an outstanding proposal to the State for constuction financing, and have applied for $1,000,000 in federal tax credits* to assist with the financing. This has been a learning process for all of us. We hope to see the project built and operating within the next year. Community House will be the only transitional rental housing in Santa Cruz, and , once built, will be the prototype for other two similar developments.

Fred, Mark and Thom labored long and hard to produce a very refined design for Community House. As it now exists, the design is essentially fixed. Community House, though representative of a major amount of work and worry, will be safe haven for all who have a chance to live within its walls.

* Which will yield $500,000.

Community House

Community House will provide 37 single-room rental units with bath-room for very-low income people, at a total cost equal to about 6 modest single family residences. In addition, Community House will have on-site laundry facilities, a large central common area, a large communal dining and meeting hall, a restaurant-quality kitchen and ample areas for sitting, reading and visiting. Bicycle parking and bus passes will be provided, as well as 15 on-site parking spaces.

Budget

Property Purchase $350,000
Misc. Development Costs $60,000
Construction Costs $1,150,00
Total Development Cost $1,560,000

Page Smith and Paul Lee celebrate with Jane Imler ending her fast upon the opening of the Cedar Street Shelter in 1985

Photo, Bill Lovejoy

Shiloh Superfly

"He who oppresses the poor insults his maker, and he who is kind to the needy honors him." Proverbs 14:31

He who mocks the poor insults his Maker, and he who rejoices at another's calamity will not go unpunished" Proverbs 17:5

He who is gracious to the poor is lending to the Lord; He will repay him for his benevolent action." Pro. 19:17

He who closes his ears to the cry of the poor will himself also cry and not be heard." Proverbs 21:13

The Cedar Street Shelter San
Lorenzo River Clean-up Crew with
Paul Lee and Page Smith

Photo, Coryo

Jan Imler and Mitch Snyder at tha Santa Cruz
Town Clock April, 1989

Photo, Coryo

Bill Tracey

Jan Freedman   *Photo, Kate Stafford*

Community House East Elevation

57

The Homeless Garden Project Crew

Photo, Paul Shraub

Top left to right

    Dan Butrica, Moonrise, Michael Walla, Bill Tracey, Daffy Maxwell,

                                        Kim Trunk, David Bennett,

Manuel Gutierrez, Josph Bader III, Judson Scoon, John Taylor,

        Adam Silverstein, Lynne Basehore, David McCall.

Chapter Seven
The Homeless Garden Project

Why I hadn't thought of it before, I can't say, but everything according to its time. Someone called from Carpenteria, California, from Paradise Herb Farm, early in 1990. Did I want a million dollars worth of herb plants? They were going out of business. "Sure. As long as I didn't have to pay for them." "Well, you'll have to pay something." "How about a tax deduction by virtue of our non-profit homeless cause?" I asked. "We might be able to work something out," they replied.   Many, many, phone calls later and a considerable shrinkdown from the original offer, we sent a truck down and picked up two thousand herb plants. It cost a thousand dollars before we were done. I could have had a better deal at the local nursery, or from my pal, Kent Taylor, who has one of the largest commercial herb gardens in California. But what the heck. I knew if we had a couple thousand plants on hand we would have to get them in the ground and we would have to have some ground to get them into; hence, the Homeless Garden Project!

I went to see my friend, Francis Corr, who runs Santa Cruz Farms, an organic truck farm. I thought a few acres adjoining his farm, on the Pogonip Park property, city land, would be a good deal and a logical site for a homeless garden project.

Francis was willing to bring in water, provide starts, and supervision. What more could you want? We walked through a little thicket behind his farm, crossed the boundary into Pogonip and there were two or three acres in a little dell. "How about here?" he said. We went to Jim Lang, Director of City Parks. "How about it?", we said. "No" he said. "No way! It's too political until we have a plan for Pogonip. But there are a couple of acres of city land adjoining a community garden down near Lighthouse Field. How about that?" We went to take a look. "I'll take it," I said, as I sniffed the ocean breezes, the air of Santa Cruz being one of my favorite phenomena. It was a block from the ocean.

We brought the herb plants over to the site and dropped them off. Remarkably, they were only a block away. We had stored them, upon arrival, in a field behind the place where *Harmony Grits* a local blue grass band, lived. They were willing to care for them until we got our garden.

Then came Arbor Day, April, 1990, and Lynne Basehore called and wanted to know if I wanted to plant a tree with the Mayor. I said, "no thanks." But she sounded so appealing and friendly, I told her about my homeless garden project. She said she was interested. She had planted trees in Malaysia. I invited her to come over and discuss the project we had in mind. A few days later, she walked in the door and Fred Gray, now our grant administrator for Community House, and I, looked at one another and raised our eyebrows and rolled our eyes in unison. We had our Director of the Homeless Garden Project.

She moved into the position, volunteering her time, for which she won the J.C. Penny Foundation "Golden Rule" Award, which carried with it a $1,000. contribution. Adam Silverstein, an environmental studies major, newly graduated from UCSC, joined the project and together they constituted the staff. We were off and running. Homeless candidates were recruited for the cause. We had a decent budget and were able to pay minimum wage for three mornings a week to our first group of homeless gardeners.

Kent Taylor, my herb grower friend, had told me about a model project in Los Angeles, run by Ida Cousino, for homeless Vietnam Vets and so we contacted Ida and asked her to come up and give us a workshop on how to do it. On a Saturday, in October, we heard about her story and how she makes about $75,000 a year selling to local restaurants. She told us we needed a celebrity to help sponsor us. It would help overcome obstacles and open doors and give us the press we needed. So, as he was my brother-in-law, an acclaimed star, and the name I love to drop, to the annoyed chagrin of my family, Harrison Ford was appealed to and kindly sent a check. We had our celebrity sponsor.

To give our initial crew some training in the Chadwick Method, I asked the staff at the UCSC Student Garden and Farm to provide some training. They were willing to do so and our first group of six went up for a number of days and learned how to double dig, compost, sow flats, and prick out seedlings into beds. It was just the backup we needed to get started. They offered to give us surplus seedlings and to send some of the apprentices down from the Agro-ecology program to help out. A new member of our staff, Jane received her training there.

A couple who are professional dowsers offered to dowse the garden, not for the purpose of finding water, but to realign the energy fields, a new use of dowsing, according to what I knew. I missed the ceremony, but was given a description of it. After all, the garden is in Santa Cruz and Santa Cruz is famous for containing practically every new age number imaginable. Why not straighten out the energy lines? I know enough about ley lines and energy centers to have some sense that there could be something to it. After the dowsing, within a week, we were given a pick-up truck, a VW bus, a van, a compost shredder, a small tractor, a roto-tiller, and a quantity of tools, as if to confirm the new energy. Some kind of energy had been straightened out. Next we're going to ask them to dowse for money.

I decided to organize a class on the garden through the cordial offices of Mike Rotkin and Community Studies at UCSC. We had a strong student input. I introduced them to the history of the Chadwick Student Garden Project at UCSC and the attendant themes relevant to the environmental crisis and the need for reaffirming the integrity of the organic. The physicalist/vitalist conflict over what counts for knowledge in the system of the sciences from the artificial synthesis of urea (1828) and the origins of 'organic' chemistry as a background for undermining the integrity of the organic was also discussed. It happens to be one of my favorite themes. I also told them of the history of homelessness in Santa Cruz, our efforts in their behalf, and the significance of voluntary associations and nonprofit corporations, as the enabling institutional instruments for community activism. The last item is another one of my favorite themes.

The first project of the class was to do this book, the history of homelessness in Santa Cruz, since the opening of the Cedar Street Shelter, in 1985. I had written an account of the Cedar Street effort, illustrated with almost all of the newspaper articles, and had circulated it privately. Now it was time to bring it up to date and make it public. Our goal was to give the citizens of Santa Cruz an accounting of what has happened in behalf of the homeless in the last six years.

We wanted to include other homeless projects, as well as our own, and give a brief description and an annual budget, but some of them refused to respond to our request. Apparently, they didn't want their budgets scrutinized. So we decided to focus on our own efforts, concentrating on the three programs under the Citizens Committee for the Homeless (the Interfaith Satellite Shelter, the Homeless Garden Project and Community House) and the two programs under the William James Association (the Free Meal Program and the proposed Homeless Resource Center). Therefore, this is only a partial picture of programs for the homeless in Santa Cruz, a picture of the work of two nonprofit agencies.

The students also worked in the garden, befriending the homeless, helping them out where they could, and engaging in fund-raising efforts. By this time, we had increased the staff. Shana Ross was in charge of foundation grants and public relations; Barbara Davis was in charge of publicity and media; Geraldine was our client services representative, dealing with all the personal problems of our workers; Robin, a professional landscape gardener, was in charge of marketing. She had expressed her interest in the project and brought Proposition C to our attention which had been passed as the Countywide Environmental Proposition, championed by Gary Patton, a County Supervisor, distinguished for his environmental leadership. We were in line to implement a number of its provisions, projects we had already undertaken, such as recycling and composting.

We had taken a field trip to Berkeley to look at a garden we had heard about on 4th Street. Just a corner lot. I had seen it on a visit to *The Gardener*, a wonderful upscale garden shop across the street. I happened to be with Virginia Baker, the Chair of the Chadwick Society. "Look at those raised bed and that intensive crop", I said. I could hardly believe my eyes. Word had it that they made over $50,000 annually, with cleaned and bagged salad greens, servicing the Berkeley restaurant market. Kona Kola Farms, it was called. They also imported fancy coffee from Hawaii. So we made a date to take the Director—Michael Norton— to lunch at Chez Panisse, the great restaurant in Berkeley, run by Alice Waters, who had been inspired by Chadwick's method of high quality food production and whom I had met at Green Gulch, the Zen farm Chadwick had originated.

An invitation to Chez Panisse was irresistible bait. We asked him to tell us his secrets. Sure enough, he had been inspired by Chadwick and the French Intensive method of high-yield, high-quality produce. He had visited the UCSC Student Garden Project as well as Glee Farms, a project I had read about with great interest in the Wall Street Journal, involving intensive gardening in greenhouses in the New York and New Jersey ghettos, a program designed to train delinquent youths in greenhouse production. I was especially interested because Glee Farms specialized in culinary herbs. He told us his whole story. He was into coffee importing, mostly just the famous one from Hawaii—Kona—hence the name of the garden. Coffee importing was seasonal; he needed something to do in the off-season. So he started the garden. They grew the most choice salad greens for the Berkeley restaurant market and yes, they made over $50,000 a year. We were overawed. A corner vacant lot in Berkeley!

He told us to go look at the composting operation down the block. We did. There was a very large lot with very large compost piles. And bins of wonderful soil—the end result of the recycling effort. They were one of a few such efforts nationally and they had designed their own machines which cost a horrendous amount of money. It was a great model for what we wanted to do albeit on a much smaller and hand-intensive scale, without the cost of the large machinery.

Then we called on Gary Patton, our leading environmentalist County Supervisor, to invite him to our class meeting. He graciously consented and gave a wonderfully impassioned talk about the reasons behind Measure C and how we could become involved in the implementation, immediately appreciating our model in terms of the opportunity for the homeless, as well as the de-centralized neighborhood hand-intensive composting and recycling effort. We were in business. He agreed to support our cause and open doors for us, including the study in process, by a major consulting firm, on how to implement Measure C, for the County of Santa Cruz. Within a month or two, he proposed over $50,000 in County funds to be granted to the Homeless Garden Project to support our effort. We eventually got $2,000. It was a tight year for the budget, although after I reviewed the budget myself, I wondered how the county could justify any number of items in the $250,000,000 indicated, such as new chairs and desks for practically everybody involved, new computers at inflated prices and so on. The only item under Homeless Grant was a copy machine at $5,000. Who got that? Our copy machine was donated by Webbers, a local firm, after one phone call. And why five times the ordinary cost? Why ask why?

Ida Cousino called and said we had to go to a meeting of the National Horticultural Therapy Association she was organizing in Palo Alto. We would be founding members of the Northern California Chapter. So we went. It was a great backup for the main focus of our work—we knew that the therapeutic aspect of our project took precedence over the economic. As long as we kept our focus on the therapeutic benefits of gardening for the homeless, the economic would follow. Or so we hoped.

At the Arbor Day Celebration of 1991, a year after meeting Lynne, the Homeless Garden Project mounted an attractive booth, with homeless gardeners and staff in attendance. We served strawberry shortcake from our first crop of strawberries, sold lettuce, and sold Homeless Garden T Shirts, which Clay Holden silkscreened for us. I handed out reprints of our "Behold Pogonip/ Greenbelt Poster", which Mark Primack designed, featuring the Sacred Oak of Santa Cruz. At noon, I lead a group to the tree in the center of Pogonip, the Sacred Oak, which we dedicated as a Heritage Tree. Now it has a nice little plaque at it's base announcing it as the Sacred Oak of Santa Cruz. I continue to do services there every Easter, Thanksgiving, and Christmas, as I have done each year since 1977.

Harrison Ford and his wife, Melissa, and mutual friends, Earl McGrath, and Bob Becker, came to visit the garden in June, while they were in Santa Cruz for Willard Ford's graduation from UCSC. Willard is my nephew. He was a student in the Homeless Garden Class and had helped me organize the class and recruit members. I was nervous about the visit, afraid of it being an imposition, due to time constraints, but it went fine. Harrison and Melissa were presented with t-shirts for the family and a box of produce and wine and coffee. Harrison planted a lemon tree which we call "the Indiana Jones Lemon Tree." He signed autographs and posed for pictures. Everyone was tickled pink. He was impressed at the amount of stuff coming up and saw immediately that it was a model for national implementation. He said he would help with publicity.

We almost ran out of money a month later and then in one week we received a grant from the Packard Foundation ($15,000 matching, which meant an eventual $30,000), a grant from the City of Santa Cruz of $5,000 and the already mentioned $2,000 from the County. Harrison called and said he would make another donation. We were out of trouble.

It is now a question of securing the future of the garden, finding new space in the event we are turned out when our lease expires in the summer of 1993, thanks to a one year renewal. Hopefully some acreage at Pogonip will be made available, a 612 acre City Park, where the homeless gardeners would be organized to develop a major botanic garden. A proposal to that effect has been made to the Pogonip Committee, recently formed to entertain project proposals for Pogonip.

Efforts are underway to develop counseling services, particularly for those with substance abuse problems, alcoholism being the most pervasive and intractable. There is some indication that the therapeutic effects of gardening is having an impact on a number of the chronic alcoholics working in the garden who are reducing their intake or stopping altogether. Some have been on the wagon for months, cold sober, after years and years of alcoholism. This, above all, demonstrates the therapeutic validity of the Homeless Garden Project and is one of the most rewarding aspects of the effort.

In early October, a Soviet television crew came to the Garden to inter-view workers and staff about the project. Ron Frazier, a San Francisco rock and roll impresario, had taken an interest in the Garden and the Chadwick Method and thought of them as models for international appli-cation, particularly in Russia. He developed a proposal called "The Global Garden" and hopes to organize a group of volunteers to travel to the Soviet Union to demonstrate the Chadwick Method and to replicate small hand intensive and high yield gardens, such as the Homeless Garden Project. Mikhail Taratuta, Bureau Chief for Soviet National Television and Radio, was impressed with the garden and the emphasis on the organic methods employed. It remains to be seen whether any funding is forthcoming to mount such an effort as a Soviet exchange which looks very unlikely.

It is all we can do at the present time to secure funding for the garden itself. We are on a short shoestring with a budget of $10,000 a month. In early October, we began an intensive fund-raising campaign with the hope of recruiting enough supporters to secure the financial future of the project.

We have constituted the *Committee of One Hundred* and the *Committee of One Thousand.* To join the *Committee of One Hundred* members are asked to pledge a monthly contribution of $25.00. Members of the *Committee of One Thousand* are asked to pledge $10 a month. If you are willing to become a member of either committee please write to Paul Lee, Box 409, Santa Cruz, California, 95061 or call 408 423 7923. I hope, as a result of reading this book, you will join with us, in our effort to end homelessness in Santa Cruz. To do so, we need your support and money, in order to continue our work. Send a check for $10.00 or $25.00 and we will sign you up for membership in the respective committee and will invoice you every month for as long as you can support our efforts. In this way, we will build a support group to sustain the programs described in this book.

Toward the end of October, the *Comic News*, a popular local newspaper featuring cartoons, included a supplement/insert on the homeless garden put together by members of the staff and the gardeners, especially Bill Tracey, one of the gardeners with excellent writing skills and Patrice Vecchione.

Lynne Basehore wrote the following Mission Statement for the Garden:

The Homeless Garden Project employs from 12-15 homeless people to grow organic produce which is sold at the Farmer's Market, at local natural food stores, and to local restaurants. The Project also recycles organic waste from three local restaurants and local landscapers by making compost with it in sixteen days.

The garden began, above all, as a safe place for homeless people. It continues under the premise of cooperation and mutual respect for the earth, the environment, and wildlife, for the community, our neighbors and their concerns for each other, our co-workers and our mutual goals; and for ourselves, our inner peace and sense of self-respect.

The garden is a context where an exchange can happen: homeless folks "producing" healthy organic food for sale and contributing to the community, and the community supporting, volunteering and keeping viable the opportunities for others.

The garden teaches us capability and compassion.

Bill Tracey wrote: *A Day In the Life of the Garden.*

The morning fog rolls in over West Cliff Drive,
muting sound and subduing color. At the Homeless
Garden Project, the flowers' bright colors are veiled
by the grey sea-mist. Later in the day the garden
will dance and sing with the purposeful activity
common to harvest time the world over, but now is
a quiet time. The workers, most of them homeless
people, are quiet, for it is early and the neighbors
are still asleep.

Nevertheless, the garden is no different from any
other agricultural enterprise. The day starts early
and the chores are never finished no matter how
long the day lasts.

With this in mind, Manny builds a fire in the grill
and sets a pot of water on the grill to heat. There is
coffee, tea, a few cakes, and some leftover sandwiches. No one need go hungry to the fields.

Manny is a quietly proud man. He is also a calmly
efficient man whose easy, shambling grace belies his
sixty years and the amount of labor he performs. As
he sips his tea, he walks the garden in his mind. He
knows each row, each bed, what's planted where and
why. He calculates what's ready for harvest and
what the approximate yield will be. Later he will
compare notes with Adam, and they will both compare their estimates to the actual yield. It is a game
they play. Manny considers the possibilities of win-
ning a few bucks betting against Adam. For an
answer, he chuckles to himself and moves off from
the fire. There are beds to be dug, weeds to be
pulled, dozens of things to be done.

The next to arrive is Bill. He is a tallish man, twenty years Manny's junior, but despite that his hair and beard are shot with grey. He walks with a limp and finds the morning fog and damp disagreeable. He and his crew will do the brunt of the landscape, carpentry and mechanical work necessary to the project. They handle the daily task of turning as much as 18 cubic yards of compost. The thought causes him to flex his back muscles until the vertebrae crackle. For breakfast, he washes down three aspirin with a cup of very hot, very strong coffee heavily laced with sugar. After a few gulps he lights a cigar. Unsurprisingly he is a former Army Sergeant.

It being harvest day, Lynne will be in. The thought causes him to smile. Lynne, the project director, is a pretty blonde woman and Bill has scar tissue almost as old as she is, but for all that, they like and respect each other and each other's devotion to the project as a whole.

Bill's train of thought is interrupted as his work partner, a rough and ready ex-carny roustabout named Skooter, arrives. Skooter kickstands his bike and fixes himself a variation of Bill's breakfast leaving out the aspirins and substituting a hand-rolled cigarette. "So what's really going on?," he asks in a voice that's about as smooth and silky as the suspension on a gravel truck.

"Ten bins to turn and a mix," Bill replies. A fifteen year veteran of the streets, the highways, the carnivals and the hobo jungles, respect does not come easily to Skooter. "Eight months on the job today. Longer than I've ever worked a job in my life." With a shrug, he walks over for a brief look at the bulletin board. A copy of the project's rules is posted there. Skooter respects the rules. He helped to make them.

A brown pickup arrives, bringing the kitchen waste from several local restaurants, a prime ingredient of our compost. Pete, the truck's driver, looks like he fell asleep at Woodstock and just woke up.

Now the arrivals come thick and fast. The pace is picking up, the energy building. Kim, tall and lank, long-haired and full-bearded, looks out at the world through thick glasses. His big hands seems so unsuited to the delicate task of seeding he finds so fascinating.

Michael, the first to admit to an abiding fondness for food, resupplies the depleted cakes.

A class of children will help harvest today. Michael will look after them. He finds it disconcerting that a government willing to spend vast sums on armaments and technology leaves it to him, poor and homeless, to educate its children on where food comes from and how. The thought gives him a certain satisfaction and he plays a little flute to chase the evil spirits away.

Joe wanders in looking like Grizzly Adams, but possessed of a talent for flower arranging and an eye for color combinations.

Dan arrives with dog and van. He will take the harvest to market. Conversations spring up that are no different from any other group of workers except these men are homeless.   They don't discuss the wife and kids or who won last night's football game. The wife and kids, if they ever had them, are somewhere back down the road and the memories of them are apt to be painful. No one owns a tv and the condition of Joe Montana's multi-million dollar arm is not of any great concern to anyone. They don't watch cop shows, they watch cops. They talk casually about who is in jail and why and are glad it's not them. They gossip about the day to day affairs of homeless people, so-and-so got drunk, or so-and-so got 86'ed from the shelter.

The sun is fully up now. The garden is filled with workers harvesting, seeding, weeding...

Boxes of produce and buckets of flowers collect at the van. The produce is washed, sorted and bunched. Bouquets are made.

Chairs and benches are pulled up. Co-eds chitchat with carny tramps. A college student planning a hiking trip gets expert advice on what does and does not belong in a backpack from a man who lives out of one. Schoolkids sort strawberries and happily munch the ones birds have pecked. There are bowls full of stirfry and peanut butter sandwiches.

And finally it's all done. The van loaded and off to market. The dishes are washed and put away. the engine on the shredder dies. Hours worked are logged in. The work area is tidied up.

One by one the workers, paid and volunteer, home-less or not, drift off. Bill mops his forehead, tosses a tarp over the shredder and relights his cigar stub. He fixes himself an evening cup of coffee, just as strong and black as the one he had for breakfast. His limp doesn't bother him and the ache in his shoulders is oddly pleasant.

Manny walks to the far end of the garden to read
the water meter and shut down the irrigation system. Even though the sun is still far above the hori-
zon, there is the beginning of a chill in the air.
Soon the fog and mist will come back. "Days getting shorter already," he says aloud to no one and
nothing in particular. He walks back to the shed
and locks the door.

The Garden has developed a program that has been tried in a number of
other communities known as Community Supported Agriculture (CSA),
offering seasonal shares of the harvest beginning in the Spring of 1992.
Consumers support a farmer who grows the produce. In return for purchasing a share of the seasonal harvest, one receives a weekly basket of fresh
produce. As a consequence of this relationship, one knows who grows the
food, where it is grown, and what methods were used in growing it.

Here is how the program works: a share is 1/120 of the Homeless
Garden Project's agricultural budget, costing $300 for the entire thirty-
five week growing season (about $8.60/week from April 1st through the
end of November). The price is calculated by dividing the total estimated
expenses incurred in growing the food, by the number of shares the garden can sustainably provide. The costs are "shared" amongst those who
will eat the "dividend", or harvest. A share is based on what one to two
people eat every week. More than one share should be purchased for
families or collective households.

It is an excellent way to guarantee part of the budget and plan for the next
season's crops.

Newsletter Spring 1992

The homeless Garden Project began two years ago as a "safe place for
homeless people to be during the day. At the time there were many people coping with the high penalties of the Camping Ban which levied fines
as high as $145 if caught sleeping in public. The streets during the day
had little to offer a tired, jobless person except further harassment and

stress. The garden attempted to offer sanctuary, a small income, and a place to regain some meaning and productivity against a backdrop of failures and catch-22's. As Kim, one of the gardener's once claimed "it was good to wake-up and know I had something to do today".

During the first year and a half The Garden has employed over 75 homeless workers, brought in over $100,000, and bridged the gap in services no longer offered by state or federal governments. Many times in the course of providing tours, offering students internships, or simply while appreciating the generous hard work of a volunteer we've asked, why can't these jobs that provide food, sustainability to the land, an sense of community be the foundation of our local economy? According to the U. S. Department of Agriculture Resource Inventory, our nation loses 4,000 to 5,000 acres of agricultural land each day. Is it any wonder that jobs, and homes are lost when the vitality of a community, it's ag lands are lost.

From the beginning the Homeless Garden Project has held a vision that returns a value of usefulness back to both our vacant lands and our marginalized peoples. We now occupy a 2.5 acre site which is one of the last remaining vacant parcels of city land. While the City is busy at work on a plan to sell the property with a subdivision of 16 single family high income houses we are actively campaigning to save the few remaining areas of prime agriculture land within the urban community. While the City hopes to make a few million from the land to offset the budgets for the next couple of years we hope to preserve the possibility of productive soil and a beautiful garden forever. Limiting growth is a difficult and controversial task. But someone has to do it. The garden has been useful to so many; the elderly neighbors, the local school kids, preschools and university interns, consumers in search of healthy food, the avid composters and naturalists, and to those who simply need to witness life's abundance, but most of all to the long term jobless and homeless citizens of this community it has been a renewal of the spirit.

Chapter Eight
The Homeless Service Center

For years, Santa Cruz has struggled to find a balance between hard economic realities and compassion for the unmet needs of the shelterless persons who reside on our streets. The devastation wrought by the Loma Prieta earthquake of 1989 brought this struggle to crisis proportions, in an upheaval that at times has threatened to tear our community apart. In 1991, two separate reports described a day resource center as a potential solution to this dilemma. The Social Issues Task Force recommended the center as a method of lessening the impact of homelessness on the downtown retail area. The Briefing Paper on Homeless Services and Service Gaps prepared by the County Human Resources Agency, in January of 1991, pointed to the center as a means to provide sanitary facilities for North County shelterless residents.

Without consistent access to sanitary facilities, the difficult journey to get off-the-streets becomes almost impossible. To find a job without access to a shower, laundry facilities, or a place to store one's belongings is an unrealistic, almost hopeless task. Employment counselors are forced to spend an inordinate amount of time attempting to provide these primary services, when their time would be much better spent preparing their clients for the real challenges that they will face in securing and maintaining employment. The difficulty of providing health care for shelterless persons becomes horribly complicated when patients are unable to clean themselves and their belongings, and lack a quiet place to recuperate during the day. Even meal operations are complicated when employees and volunteers are unable to find access to sanitary facilities. By creating a centralized location for direct service provision, many existing services will become more effective.

In March, the Coalition for a Safe Place to Sleep submitted an application for funding from 1991 Community Development Block Grants (CDBG). At this time, the management of A Free Meal, under the auspices of the William James Association, submitted a proposal for the Homeless Resource Center, a more detailed and final version of the Coalition's original application for funding.

The Resource Center would be a multi-purpose service center designed to address the unmet primary service needs of homeless people in the City of Santa Cruz. The facility would be available to homeless people seeking a variety of services: storage, hygiene care, information and referral, phone and mail contact. Additionally, the center will be a safe and legal location for homeless people to gather, come in off the streets, and be in a position to access social and other services available to them.

The Center will serve as an outreach location for the many existing homeless support programs. The Homeless Employment Program, the Homeless Garden Project, the Homeless Persons' Health Project, and the Mobile Outreach Support Team are examples of the groups which would be provided with regularly scheduled hours of operation. A Free Meal will be absorbed into the overall structure of the center, and the site will serve as the pickup spot for the Interfaith Satellite Shelter Program.

Currently, a site selection committee consisting of homeless service providers, City Council members, appropriate technical consultants, and homeless persons is working to develop a site and implementation plan for the Resource Center. Since the exact operational details and hours of operation will depend greatly on the site chosen, at this time we can only indicate ideal levels of service.

> *Storage of belongings:* we will provide a minimum of 150 lockers, of the size necessary to store a large backpack.

> *Showers:* we would like to provide two showers each for males and females. To practise water conservation, low-flow shower heads should be installed, as well as a system of tokens and time meters. Two sets

of two low-flush toilets should be sufficient.

Phones: one line should be available for administrative use. One line should be available for incoming calls only, with a pay phone installed for return calls. A system will be established for reliable relaying of phone messages.

Mail: shelterless persons should be able to receive mail at the Center's address. A reliable system of mail distribution will be the responsibility of the Director.

Laundry: two sets of washer/dryers will be on site and available for use all day.

Meal Service: coffee, juice, and donated cold snacks will be served all day as donations allow. A hot meal will be provided each night, consistent with the current level of service of A Free Meal.

Outreach: a quiet, separate area will be provided for other service providers. The Director will work with all groups to schedule regular, convenient outreach hours.

Organized along the lines of A Free Meal, the Service Center Director would be responsible for all fund-raising, bookkeeping, and community relations work. The Director would also have oversight responsibility for day-to-day program operation, and for the hiring and firing of staff members. All employees will be drawn from the homeless community, with current employees of A Free Meal guaranteed at least an equivalent amount of hours as they have at the time of the transition. The Director will supervise all employees, who will in turn coordinate volunteers in their areas. The entire community is responsible for enforcing all program rules. The use of alcohol or drugs will not be allowed on the premises, and violence, theft, or severe disruptions will not be tolerated.

Decisions will be made in weekly community meetings, ideally reaching consensus but voting when consensus is not reached. One of the first tasks of the community meetings will be to determine what the consequences will be when rules are violated.

The Homeless Community Resource Center will fill a crucial gap in the current network of homeless services. It will relieve all other service providers from the burden of locating primary hygiene care for their clients, and allow them to better use their resources to provide their specialized services.

For the Homeless Employment Program, the Center will mean that job applicants can be clean, wear laundered clothes, and store their belongings while they work. It will enable their clients to receive phone messages quickly, and to be waiting at a central location should casual labor be available. The Program will also provide invaluable support to homeless employees of the Center.

The Homeless Persons' Health Project will be able to provide outreach at an indoor, clean, central location. Those who are ill, but not seriously enough to be hospitalized, will have a quiet place to rest and recover. The Health Project will also be able to act as an advisory body on health-related aspects of community living at the Center.

The Mobile Outreach Support Team operated by Supportive Outreach Services provides excellent support for those with mental health concerns. Through this team, shelterless persons are put in touch with Pioneer House. This drop-in center for the mentally ill is able to provide for almost all of the needs of their clients. It is hoped that the team will provide regular outreach at the Resource Center.

County Mental Health has expressed a willingness to schedule regular case management hours at the Center. This will provide a crucial link between the mental health system and those clients on the streets. Many shelterless persons are entitled to benefits they are not aware of, and outreach is desperately needed to enable these persons to enter the mental health system.

The Center will serve as the pickup site for the Interfaith Satellite Shelter Program. Since Satellite hours extend beyond the expected operating hours of the Center, ISSP will assume the financial responsibility for staffing the Center from six p.m. through eight p.m. each evening.

The Free Meal program and all associated costs would be absorbed into the overall structure of the Resource Center.

For years it had been obvious to anyone who worked with the homeless that a day center was desparately needed in Santa Cruz. Unfortunately, the consensus among the powers that be was either: no one would use it; or, homeless people the world over would converge on Santa Cruz to use it. So, the idea was immediately nixed anytime it was brought up.

In the homeless hysteria following the earthquake, Vision Santa Cruz recommended reviving the "Downtown Social Issues Task Force", (or "The How To Run The Bums Out Of Town Committee",) but with the addition of a few liberals to balance things out, or at least add a little 'pull' to the 'push'. Thanks to the help of Mary Thurwachter from Legal Aid, and a few others who probably wouldn't want to be publicly thanked, they squeezed Karen Gillette on at the last moment as part of the services subcommittee, with Bob Campbell, the current administrator of the River Street Shelter and Will Lightbourne of Human Resources Agency. Although Karen secretly felt that HRA stood for "Human Regulatory Agency", she immediately liked and trusted Will and HRA's homeless analyst, Judy Schwartz. They both had a pragmatic and honest way of laying things right on the line that she appreciated.

Karen knew that if the basically conservative task force recommended a day center, it would be pretty easy to get the City Council to approve it. At first it seemed hopeless, because one Downtown Association member couldn't cope with the concept of doing anything for the homeless, only to them. But somehow, Will talked them into a lukewarm recommendation and they were on their way.

At first, the cause was championed by the Coalition For A Safe Place To Sleep. They had done an amazing job of generating community support for the homeless during attempts to get a campground a few months before. A Free Meal seemed to be the obvious choice of management for the Center since they spent less money than everyone else and had more fun doing it. Of course, the big question was "where can we put it?"

At first, ideas ran toward modular units on temporary sites, which didn't appeal to them very much since they had been "temporary" since the day they opened and were kind of sick of it. Next, someone floated the idea of sharing the River Street Shelter building, which struck terror into their hearts!

Economically it made sense, but logistically it was a nightmare. The energy of the meal depends on the homeless knowing that they "own" the program, and they could never "own" River Street!

Just when the process felt doomed, Harriett Deck, of Schooner Realty, arrived on the scene like a fairy godmother to help them lease the building next door to the Free Meal site. As they watched, she calmly began to help them "control their own destiny" in a somewhat miraculous way. The owner wasn't interested in leasing the site- the only way they could have it was by purchasing the entire building. Of course, this seemed impossible, but before true hopelessness set in, Harriett had enlisted the help of Housing For Independent People (H.I.P.), a non-profit developer who was already involved in the Community House project.

As they stood back in amazement, Harriett, and H.I.P. representatives, Al DiLudovico and Thom McCue, took on the task of buying the building so they could lease it. It was as if someone had sent in the proverbial knight on a white horse!

As if this help wasn't more than they had imagined possible, the City of Santa Cruz allocated almost $225,000. toward the Day Center out of Community Development Block Grant (CDBG) funds to get the Center up and running. They had to keep pinching themselves to make sure they were awake and still in Santa Cruz!

Then, just when the financing of the building seemed most grim the

County of Santa Cruz stepped in to make the fairy-tale complete. In a rather complex arrangement between the County, the City and HIP, over $800,000 in bond money has been set aside to finance the project. For a group born out of utter cynicism at the way Santa Cruz handled homelessness, they were amazed at what the grownups could do when they put their minds to it.

Karen Gillette comments on her experience:

"To see so many different parts of our community pitch in to make our dream a reality was the most wonderful reinforcement of our original philosophy of seeing everyone as potentially helpful, not as potential stumbling blocks. We owe our deepest gratitude to so many people- to the Coalition For A Safe Place To Sleep, who created the atmosphere for it all to happen in, to Hariett, Thom, and Al, for giving us a level of professionalism that we never dreamed of, to Will Lightbourne and Judy Schwartz, for their endless support and pep talks, to the City Council for getting behind homeless services in such a big way, to the Board of Supervisors, especially Fred Keeley, for bailing us out of the real estate blues, and most especially to Don Lane, who keeps saying "we" instead of "you". In a place where there's only "us", Don fits right in!"

Hopefully, the Day Center will open in 1992.

Chapter Nine
The Future of Homelessness and the Possibility of a Solution

What is the future of homelessness? More homeless? In this morning's paper, we read: "U. S. cities have more hungry and homeless people than they can feed and house and the situation is getting worse, the U. S. Conference of Mayors said yesterday." (San Francisco Chronicle, Dec. 17, 1991).

No one wants to talk about a solution to homelessness. It is a limiting concept for the imagination. I felt deep resistance whenever I brought up the subject, even among colleagues, just for possible discussion, as if my imaginative (and enthusiastic) excess was exposed at its worst point. There he goes thinking about solutions when there is no possibility of one. Might as well work on a cure for cancer.

It was unacceptable to think of homeless people sleeping on church floors for the rest of time in spite of what it did for the morale of the churches. Band-aid solutions were short term. We had to think about the long haul. We had to be the first community in the United States to solve the problem. Why not? We were to scale. Problems were not outsized for us as they were in greater metropolitan communities. I took one hundred homeless as my starting point. It was the number we supported in our Interfaith Satellite Program for the first few years The number rose to over one hundred and twenty-five in 1991-2, in terms of the nightly maximum average. This was partly due to the fact that we had extended the program county wide, including Watsonville.

I have no idea how many homeless there are in Santa Cruz County, although the estimate has been given at 2,000. But I am willing to help find a solution for a hundred. I thought about selling my home. Theoretically, that is. I knew my wife wouldn't go for it, even theoretically, but it provided me with an example of the problem. At the time, I could have sold it for $400,000, although the recent decline in the real estate market has lowered the value. (I paid $33,500 in 1967). It would pay for apartments for my one hundred homeless for one year. One house against shelter for one hundred homeless for one year! I had the most glaring example of the discrepancy in affordable housing in our community.

At one point, we had the chance to consider renting or buying and moving into the Greenwood Lodge. Page Smith and I went out to take a look at it. It was for sale. An old left wing radical camp in the woods above Capitola. All we needed was a million. Page rolled his eyes. It would have created an instant homeless community for one hundred or more. The beds were all made in the thirty or forty cabins. There was a large lodge with an institutional kitchen. There was a campsite above the compound on a plateau, possibly enough room for another hundred. There was a swimming pool. But it was remote, stuck off in the country, difficult to get to, and the timing was off. Now it is the world headquarters for the Dalai Lama. He needed it more than we did. Instead, we will sink a million into Community House for forty. But it is close to town, behind the shelter and next to what looks like the future site of the service center. We have our centralized complex intact.

The present possibility for an instant community, with accommodations for over one hundred is Beulah Park, an almost abandoned former fundamentalist bible camp, just outside of Santa Cruz, off Highway 17, before Pasatiempo. Lots of cabins, most of them falling down, a large kitchen, a huge quonset type auditorium, which is condemned, although the earthquake didn't seem to bother it. Lots of space in terms of land, although some of it falls off into a deep ravine. I reeled away in abject disgust at the deteriorated condition of the place, not wanting to put my worst enemies there, although a few came to mind.

Then I got over my reaction and realized it was the very reason for getting it for the homeless. No one else would touch it with a thousand foot pole. We could fix it up. We know of the availability of rehab money from the State. We put together a coalition to prepare the way: The Homeless Action Network, although the Homeless Service Center was an immediate concern. After the service center, we could turn our attention to a large scale homeless community with low cost housing and wave our magic wand.

After all, when you look at the accomplishments over the last seven years, there is no reason to believe an end is not in sight. But for the recession, which no one at present can fathom. Perhaps we are headed for hard times beyond our imagining—the grapes of wrath may be upon us once more.

What is needed is a reform of the social services system in this country, in this state (California) and in this county (Santa Cruz). Without this reform, we have to fight against an entrenched bureaucracy almost incapable of an original idea on their own and bent upon thwarting those who come up with one, although this is beginning to change under the current welfare administration and their attention to homeless services. There are sufficient resources and there is available space. Take one simple fact. Not a single high school or grade school gymnasium is open to the homeless on any given night during the year in this county. Why not? If the churches of the community can do it why not the schools? Physical plants abound. Getting into them is another matter. This is true in every community in the land.

While teaching Ethics at Cabrillo College in the Spring Semester of l991, I spent some time reviewing the history of homelessness as a case study in ethics. I invited the Santa Cruz County Director of Human Resources— Will Lightbourne—to talk to the class about his views and the agency's views on homelessness. I warned him that I would be especially critical of the General Assistance Program, the bottom rung of the welfare dollar, and would ask him a number of critical questions about this objectionable underbelly of the welfare system, as I found myself calling it, once I found out how it operated. He said, "o.k."; he was willing to discuss it.

I had heard about General Assistance when I decided to help a homeless fellow, who, one night, at one of our church sites, approached me and asked me if I knew of a half-way house for ex-cons. I knew of none in Santa Cruz. I asked the next question: Was he an ex-con? Not exactly. He was running from the law over the issue of mistaken identity. He was confused with a man who had murdered two women in Santa Cruz and he had been stopped in five or six states, arrested, and jailed, until it could be determined that his fingerprints did not match those of the murder suspect, when he would be released, only to have his license plate noticed by the next patrol, when he would be picked up again. You know, a computer glitch. They even suspected he had altered his fingerprints which was why they didn't match those of the murder suspect.

He had been arrested eight times as Gary Partlow, in Colorado, Nevada, Oregon and California.

As I looked at this bearded fellow, I had the sneaking suspicion that I was beholding the most abject human being in Santa Cruz. He was the candidate for the negative prize—bankrupt on the wheel of fortune. There was something about him that made me think I had better help him even though he didn't have a clubfoot. I told him I would help him. I knew about General Assistance as the bottom rung of the welfare dollar. It was the response of the County of Santa Cruz to emergency need of the most dire kind. If you were penniless, down on your luck, stuck in town, out of gas, not a dime, nothing to eat, no where to sleep—you were eligible for GA. Now wait a minute! Isn't this a description of the homeless? Isn't everyone who is homeless a candidate for GA? Well, let's not make a category mistake. We're talking about this poor soul in front of me, not about the homeless in general. His name was Hoffman. I told him I would help him get through GA. I have to admit, I was looking for a guinea pig. I had heard about the program and I wanted to know how it worked. I would track Mr. Hoffman through the maze. He would be my learning experience. I would find out why the homeless in general didn't apply or weren't eligible for GA. I would see for myself why this was the objectionable underbelly of the welfare system.

Well, needless to say, he didn't make it through the system. I didn't know it then, but I know it now—the program is designed to *wear you out*.

Tillich makes the point about the quickness of response to need, as one of the critical features of a philosophy of social welfare. Good luck. I found out they *deliberately* make you wait two weeks before they give you any money in the hope you will go away and take your need with you. I should have given Hoffman out-of -pocket money. I did it in any number of other instances. I just didn't think of it probably because he didn't ask. Three days into the process he stole a piece of bologna from a local Safeway store and was arrested. He called me from jail. "Hello, Mr. Lee. This is Hoffman. I'm in jail." "Not another mistaken identity," I asked. "No, bologna."

I wondered about this guy. Why had he come to Santa Cruz, the very place of the murders he was confused with, like some kind of perverse magnetic draw? I may have asked him, but I don't remember what he said. I repressed my suspicions and took him at his word. He was so beleagured and abject, so hounded and down on his luck he needed emergency help no matter what his story was. He had all the earmarks of the proverbially drowning rat.

I learned enough from his example to confirm my worst fears about General Assistance. He had mentioned on his GA form a bank account in Nevada where he had $14.00 in savings. GA wanted an affadavit from the bank to that effect. That was a good one. He had to get three different estimates on his car from three different garages, indicating it was not worth more than $500. He didn't have any gas and he had no money to buy any. That was another good one. And on and on. How much would Mr. Hoffman have received in his emergency state had he been declared eligible after the two weeks or more of forms and interviews? $110. A month. This is a loan. It has to be paid back out of the first paychecks in the event of getting a job. Every week you have to list ten places you have applied for a job when every case worker knows these are made up which means complicity in lying.

There is a lien on the loan. A what? A lien. You mean "lean", as in "lean on me", in terms of the whole system wanting to crush you? No. A lien against any future property you may ever own. Who? Hoffman? It was ludicrous. The lien was just to shove your face in it: a lien on the loan against any possible future property! The word "mendacious" came to mind again. I actually went to the dictionary and looked it up. It means lying, untrue, spurious, false. Deception. In other words, you go to a social agency in the utmost need, absolutely down on your luck, your tongue hanging out, and they are supposed to help you with the law of listening love. Ha ha. Sure. We're talking General Assistance. We're talking mendacity. We're talking about lying deception on the part of a social service agency theoretically devoted to human welfare.

I got so mad I went to the Grand Jury. I had a friend who was sitting on it. I told her about the Hoffman case. She said call up and make an appointment. I did. I stated that I had a case of welfare fraud. You know, mendacity. I meant the system, not some poor single ethnic mother on the fraud hook. They all looked at me with a little twist to their necks. I described the General Assistance Program. They clucked. Bad enough, but where's the fraud? 75% of the money goes to administer it. For every dollar given, it costs $ .75 cents to give it. That's fraud. *They pay people to see to it that those in need don't get it!* That's mendacious! They didn't believe me, but they said they would investigate. It turned out to be true. I had Grand Jury confirmation, but that's as far as it went. It was mentioned in their Annual Report for 1987/88.

So now I had Will Lightbourne, the Director of the Human Resources Agency, in class, recently appointed to the job and for all extents and purposes representing a new point of departure. He was terrific. A Jamaican. Very smooth, very impressive, very cool, but with lots of heart. He had come out of Catholic Charities to head the County Welfare Agency known as Human Resources. He gave a brief rundown on the burdens of the agency. We were all immediately depressed by his account. How can anyone handle such a job all along the line? The described need was so great. He talked about people running down the corridors, the case load is like that, the time is so short, the needs are so severe. We said how about introducing volunteers—I had students in the class ready to raise their hands—to help with the pressure. He said, no way, the union wouldn't allow it. Uh huh.

So much of the budget went to families with dependent children

(AFDC)—I forget the budget figure, but I perked up when he said: "we can cut a check for AFDC applicants in two hours". "Oh, oh", I thought, "Wait till we get to the General Assistance lag". On and on—food stamps, child abuse, health, refugees, vets, public guardian, foster care, adoption, adult services, you name it, need upon need, all into hysterical overload. We finally got to GA. He smiled a wry smile and agreed with everything I said. "It's not my design, you have to understand, and I have to live with it." Why?, I thought, people take out the garbage once a week. They trap rats. They report noisy neighbors to the police. There are all kinds of things we don't have to live with.

Mr. Lightbourne continued: "Well, the State has been talking about taking over the program so its days may be numbered in terms of local administration. The money comes out of the General Fund of the County. It is the toughest dollar. You're right. The whole system is designed, at the level of GA, to see to it that as few people as possible get it." He admitted it. "We make them wait two weeks. We can cut a check for AFDC (aid to families with dependent children) in two hours. With GA, it is routine. It is policy." Hearing it again didn't make it sink in any deeper.

I had the terrible admission. But it was only over coffee after the class that I found out the bottom line. Why this squeeze on GA when it is supposed to be the emergency need program? It should be the most responsive and the most receptive to need. Because the image of the GA client is what? The homeless? No, it is worse than that. Tighter than that? What? What image is worse than the homeless, most of whom are in genuine need? The Deadhead! Oh, come on! Yes, the Deadhead! The image in the community of Santa Cruz of the person who applies for GA is the Deadhead. I suddenly realized that if he didn't share this perceived image he had acquiesced to it.

Immediately, I understood that Deadheads, the notorious followers of the Grateful Dead, the psychedelic band of the 60s, still running strong, every performance a sell-out, was the excuse for *not* responding to emergency need—the Deadhead was the image hovering over the GA program. Don't give them the money, because they don't deserve it! Those

Deadheads! They aren't really in need. They're on their way to the next concert where they can smoke dope and drop acid and sell their beaded jewelry crap.

They *want* to be out there in la-la land. They *want* to be on the hand-out. They *want* to be homeless, living out of their van, if they have one. They *want* their chosen way of life. They have repudiated the American Way of Life. They are critics of it! They don't want to work from 9 to 5. Why should we give our hard-earned tax dollars to the Deadheads? Why, indeed?!

I thought of Hoffmann.

It was the homeless male that was most hurt by this stigma of the Deadhead.

As Peter Marin states it in his article in *The Nation:* "The Prejudice Against Men", it is homeless men who are the most neglected because men are not supposed to need help:

> *To put it simply: Men are neither supposed nor allowed to be dependent. They are expected to take care of others and themselves. And when they cannot do it, or 'will not' do it, the built-in assumption at the heart of the culture is that they are less than men and therefore unworthy of help. An irony asserts itself: Simply by being in need of help, men forfeit the right to it.*

The homeless male was a Deadhead.

I found out that the budget for GA was over $400,000 a year. $200,000 went to administer it. I had the solution in a flash. "Mr. Lightbourne," I said, "we will arrange for the Grateful Dead to play Santa Cruz once a year and we will raise $400,000 from a single concert, just your budget for General Assistance."

I had thought about starting a nonprofit GA, as a community effort, funded with $100,000, the amount that went to recipients, administered by volunteers. We'd show them. After a demonstration year, where we would spend less than ten per cent on administration, we would contract for the GA budget and see to it that almost all the money went to those in emergency need. We would force the hand of the County on the delivery of the emergency welfare dollar. I would come to realize that this was one of my more naive and unrealizable ideas.

So here I was offering a check to Mr. Lighbourne, as the result of an imagined Grateful Dead Benefit for GA, in the amount of his annual budget. He did not extend his hand. "We wouldn't accept it", he said, without hesitation.

I was dumbfounded. "Why not?"

"Don't you understand? We don't want to give money to Deadheads!"

The image suited me in my worst moods in thinking about the homeless. I remembered my first impression when I went down to help at Peter Carota's kitchen. I thought I had entered a scene from Dante—you know—"abandon all hope ye who enter here". I thought this is the night of the living dead, only it's not a movie. These guys are living it. What I meant was that this perception of the homeless was the perception of the middle class, the propertied, those with a home, my own first impression. I was looking into a mirror in the sense of *seeing my own perception*, rather than looking straight and true at fellow human beings in need. The homeless were the living dead, lurking around outside, waiting to get into the kitchen to steal a beer and then anything else they could lay their hands on. Any minute now, a greedy, ugly hand will break through the window. They were a threat to one's bourgeois security. The homeless were the *un*-grateful dead! They had ceased to exist because they were unemployed and lacked shelter. Therefore, they were as good as dead. They were less than human. They were ghouls. The metaphor fulfilled itself. It was the meaning of "disappearance" applied to the homeless. They had departed from humanity—from all those who had jobs and homes to go home to with loved ones waiting and a hot meal on the table. And they returned as though from the dead to haunt the bourgeois and to make them uncomfortable to the depths of their bourgeois souls.

And now it was clear: The image of the Deadhead, that counter-culture critic of bourgeois values and meaning, the threat to the American Way of Life, the turned-on dropped-out member of the Timothy Leary gang, who tuned in to the endless riffs of Jerry Garcia and his band, the hippy of old, going back to U.T.E.'s, which stood for the Undesirable Transient Element, which is what the community of Santa Cruz called them in the 60s and 70s, the hippy-Deadhead was the excuse for witholding the welfare dollar from the neediest of the neediest in the County of Santa Cruz.[3]

To quote Peter Marin again:

> *Whatever particular griefs men may have*
> *experienced on their way to homelessness, there is one*
> *final and crippling sorrow all of them share: a sense of*
> *betrayal at society's refusal to recognize their needs. Most*
> *of us—men and women—grow up expecting that when*
> *things go terribly wrong someone, from somewhere, will*
> *step forward to help us. That this does not happen, and*
> *that all watch from the shore as each of us, in isolation,*
> *struggles to swim and then begins to sink, is perhaps the*
> *most terrible discovery that anyone in society can make.*
> *When troubled men make that discovery, as all homeless*
> *men do sooner or later, then hope vanishes completely;*
> *despair rings them round; they have become what they*
> *need not have become: the homeless men we see every-*
> *where around us.*

The moral of the story was clear—it was impossible to expect from established agencies what they were unable or unwilling to give—the response to the homeless would have to come from the private sector of volunteers and nonprofit corporations, exactly according to our experience over the last six years, although even there we had to learn a lesson.

We came to realize that certain nonprofits mirrored the established agencies. The established and successful nonprofits, that is, the big ones—were professionals with a track record. There was a kind of collusion operating even at the nonprofit level, in league with City and County agencies, although this was seeing it from a particular point of view: ours. We gave our time freely, without pay. No one at the Board of Director's level received any pay, although we had a fairly large (under) paid staff running our programs. We had no Executive Director and staff to run the programs above the program directors themselves. The professional nonprofits were heavily stacked with well-paid administrators; hence, the inflated budgets. This was understandable. It was their job. But we wondered about the lack of scrutiny over these budgets and the tendency to float larger and larger budgets every year for seemingly less and less services. It looked like the routinization of charisma all over again, that old Max Weber theme. You get the spontaneous response from people with the spirit to do it, whatever the demand is, and then the more organized, the more administration is needed, the more bureaucratized, the more routinized, and the spirit departs, as though on schedule. The current United Way scandal is a good example of skimming money for bloated salaries and perks at the top.

I can imagine the routinization syndrome happening to us in a decade, but for our effort to turn the operation of programs over to the homeless themselves, moving them up to staff levels and positions of responsibility, where the talent and ability many of them have can be demonstrated, as, in our experience, it always was. You could count on it. It was part of the internal morale that working together in a common cause necessarily produced. Maybe this avowed aim would keep the spirit moving.

Millions of dollars are being spent on the homeless every year in Santa Cruz. It is something approaching an industry. Not even the generosity of local contributions has been tapped out. We have a good model to show for our half decade work in the five programs detailed here. The Garden has proved to be the most promising from the point of view of rehabilitation. Chronic alcoholics and drug users get another chance to try to kick their dependency with all the support the project can muster. People who will never hold a conventional job take to gardening as if it were made just for them. There is something awesome about the produc-

tivity and fertility of the cultivated land that is therapeutic and transforming, when the corn you have planted is as high as an elephant's eye. There
is comraderie and a sense of increasing morale even in the face of adversi-
ty. They aren't going to let their stuff, what they have planted, die. So
they themselves take strength, accordingly. They live and grow to make
live and grow. Healthy people follow healthy plants as a matter of course.

Part of the problem is the attribution of homelessness to a group of people, which thereby stigmatizes them. It is a kind of double bind. First of all
you have no home to call your own and then you are called "homeless" as
if to fix you in your predicament. How can someone who is homeless get
a home? Part of the intractability of this predicament is the label; once
homeless, it is almost impossible to overcome one's plight. One has fall-
en between the cracks. We worried about this when we thought about
calling our project—"The Homeless Garden Project." Wasn't this
another fix? How would we get the homeless gardeners out of their
predicament if they were labelled homeless? We live in a society that cat-
egorizes with a vengeance. You're supposed to wear your label on your
sleeve. What do you do for a living? What are you? Who are you? A
salesman, a doctor, a lawyer, a teacher, a cleaning lady, a whatever. We
are defined by our jobs and our positions, instead of our being. Being?
That's too abstract. Make something of yourself and then be called by it,
or else, which is roughly tantamount to "get a job".

My initial thought, when we opened the Cedar Street Shelter, was this
question of identity and how to shake the stigma of homelessness. I
thought of starting a local chapter of the California Conservation Corps;
after all, we had helped get the State Corps started in 1976 as it was one of
our original aims in starting the William James Association. The Smiths
were in Jerry Brown's office when he announced in his State of the State
Address that there would be a California Conservation Corps. We were
invited in on the ground floor and Brown takes pains to credit us with the
idea. Why not start a corps for the homeless— The Santa Cruz
Conservation Corps. Give everyone in the shelter a shirt and a patch
identifying them as members of the corps. Instantly, they would have a
new identity, a purpose in life, projects to develop and execute and a solidarity, one with the other.

We went so far as to organize a clean-up campaign for the banks of the San Lorenzo River—some of the members of the shelter actually proposed it after they heard our talk about the C.C.C. They wanted to do something for the downtown community. We went out and picked up trash and refuse on a Saturday. We got our pictures in the paper. It was a good experience. But that was as far as it went.

Recently, I saw a program on NBC News, describing a program called ACCION International, with headquarters in Cambridge, Mass. Begun in l961, ACCION is known as banker to the poor, creating employment and economic opportunities in the Americas, mostly South America, with small loans, very small. Defining themselves as a private sector Peace Corps, ACCION made its first loans to small businesses in l973 in Recife, Brazil. This experiment in grass-roots capitalism proved so successful that by l980, ACCION had decided to make lending the main focus of its program. Funding comes from donations and low-interest loans by foundations, corporations and individuals.

The Ford Foundation recently awarded ACCION a $2 million seven year loan at l% interest. The loan is made to micro-entrepreneurs. The average loan is $l25, just about the amount of the General Assistance 'loan'. The difference is that almost every single loan is paid back, so keen are the borrowers to establish a good credit history. $38 million in loans is made to more than 67,000 of the smallest-scale businesses, generating over 30,000 new jobs. More than half the loans are made to women. The loans, which are accompanied by management training and technical assistance, allow entrepreneurs to buy goods and raw materials in bulk or purchase machines to boost output, freeing borrowers from usurious rates charged by loan sharks.

Can we translate this program to a community such as Santa Cruz and apply it to the homeless, the candidates for General Assistance? As well as hiring the homeless and having to raise the money to maintain a growing budget, such as the minimum wage salaries for the Homeless Garden Program, loans could be made to help develop cottage industry type employment, based on the industry and initiative of those who apply. It is possible that such cottage industry efforts can be organized out of the

Homeless Resource Center.

It could be that we are stuck in a rut that is only going to get deeper and deeper as times get harder and harder and more and more need piles on need already perceived and goes begging. The homeless problem is worsening. There is no question about that. And no end in sight. And none of us are equal to the task.

Mr. Lightbourn read a draft of the book and wrote me a letter which I include here. It is an example of two different perceptions responding to the same problem. I could have corrected what I wrote in the light of what he says but I thought it better to let him speak for himself and let the reader respond to the two different versions of the same story.

> County of Santa Cruz
> Human Resources Agency
> Will Lightbourne, Administrator
> 1000 Emeline St.
> Santa Cruz, Ca. 95060
>
> February 8, 1992
>
> Dear Paul:
>
> Judy Schwartz gave me a copy of the manuscript of "The Quality of Mercy." Although I normally hate to get between an artist and his work, I do feel the need to pick a few nits with you.
>
> First, some points regarding General Assistance:
>
> We've been over this before, but apparently need to look at the dollars again. In FY (fiscal year) 1990/1991, we issued approximately $640,000 in G.A. payments to clients. Our costs for administering the program were slightly under $200,000. The latter

figure is the salaries and benefits of four workers, all office and operating costs, G.A.'s share of Fair Hearings and Fraud costs (which cannot be charged to the State and Federally-funded welfare programs), and County overhead (a pro-rata share of what things like County Counsel, Auditor, Information Services, etc., charge the direct service agencies.)

It is *not* G.A. policy to delay payments by any period of time. It is a result of the small staff and their workload. In the current fiscal year I have added a staff position to the program to try and cut the backlog. In fact, G. A. clients usually receive Food Stamps on the day of application, and applicants are scheduled as quickly as possible for full interviews for G.A. As a coincidental result of the delays that sometimes occur, however, we do find that a significant proportion of the employable applicants do not keep their appointments and do not appear — I would speculate that these are people who obtained work or were transients.

"It's not my design...." Please keep in mind that I had been at HRA about seven months when I addressed your class in 1991. Since then we have added staff, reorganized the employable part of the program to provide Work Adjustment Training (essentially, paid on-the-job experiences equal to the G.A. payment, plus supportive services and supplies) for those recipients whose barriers to employment seem so profound as to keep them permanently in the dependency system. We have also formally changed the residency requirement to more realistically meet the needs of homeless recipients. These changes have all been endorsed by Legal Aid.

No funds for Deadheads: You will recall that I

explained to your class that about 85% of the G.A. recipients were pending disability cases, and of the remaining 15%, most were people with short-term problems that necessitated one or two months of aid. I did, however, say that a few applicants were people who were very clear that they did not want to participate in the work world. I then asked your class two questions:

One I suggested four hypothetical clients — the evidently physically or mentally disabled person awaiting action on an SSI application; the self-employed tree-trimmer with a broken arm and no unemployment benefits; the late stage alcoholic who might or might not be SSI-eligible, but who was clearly incapable of keeping a job; and, the able-bodied person who didn't want to deal with the "authority" of the job-place.

My question was this: You are both the voters of Santa Cruz County (my bosses), and the people who are providing the money I distribute in G.A. Who do you want me to give the money to?

Virtually the entire class of 30 or so indicated we should give G.A. to the first two people; a few wanted to give money to the alcoholic; and no hand (including yours) was raised for the last person..

My response to the class (and you) was that we would give G.A. to all of them. However, for the first person we would do whatever we could to get them on SSI quickly. For the second person, we wouldn't sweat it, because we know he would be a one- or two-month client. For the third, we would try to get a disability diagnosis and/or try to get him into a residential program. And for the fourth, we would insist that he conduct a weekly job search and would follow-up to make sure he had done so.

No, Paul, I do *not* see our G.A. clients as being Deadheads. However, we do have a few applicants who might fit that label, and I equally do not think that it is the taxpayer's responsibility to underwrite a counter-culture. I believe we are, to the extent we are physically and mentally able, responsible for ourselves. And to the extent that people are physically or mentally limited, we are our brother's — and our sister's — keepers. Your class evidently agreed with me... and then some.

Two After reviewing the gaps and shortcoming in the public welfare and social service system, I asked your class: Imagine that you are the Santa Cruz welfare director, and imagine also that someone says "here's and extra $250,000—spend it where you want to," where would you spend it? Almost all said they would spend it on Child Protective Services, a few said AFDC, and none said G.A. As I recall, you said nothing. It is an old axiom of Roman Law that silence gives consent.

If I had an extra $100,000 or $1,000,000 G.A. is not where I would put it. I would put it into social services and emplyment services. The reason I would not put it in G.A. is *not* because I don't like the G.A. clients, but because G.A. payments are not awarded according to how much money is available. In FY 1990/1991 we overspent the G.A. budget by nearly 150% and no-one—Board, CAO, whomever— objected. We spend according to who is eligible, and in recession years that will almost certainly result in spending over budget. Please bear in mind that every G.A. applicant has recourse to Fair

Hearing if they feel they have been unfairly denied or discontinued, and in my experience, the Fair Hearing decisions split about equally.

The other area I want to comment on is your view of our homeless work. You take issue with our emphasis on case-management and transitional housing (although, evidently, see the parallel Homeless Day Resource Center, which was conceived during the same process, as coming accompanied by a burning bush.)

First, I regret you didn't raise these concerns with me while we were developing the plan. Paul Pfotenhauer, Karen Gilette, and Andrew Morin were all extensively consulted during its development...and all supported it. I assumed that meant the Citizens Committee and William James was in support — again, perhaps, an over-reliance on Roman Law. I also think you will find that Karen will credit HRA with unstinting support of making the Day Center a reality.

You seem to be dismissing our plan as something which is just words and will now disappear. In fact, the first transitional housing for North County was acquired a few weeks ago, and should be rehabilitated and open within a few months. A broader voucher-based transitional system should also be operating within that timeframe. The case management should also come on line in that period. Again, if you disagree with our services that is certainly your right, but it feels a little mean-spirited to just assume that it is a paper exercise; I would certainly give your and similar organizations more credit for your intentions than you seem willing to give in return.

Finally, one small, personal moan. While I appreciate the nice things you said about me personally, my teeth grate on the word "bureaucrat". For seven years, before HRA, I was director of Catholic Charities of the Archdiocese — an operating budget of $12 million, a housing development budget of about $10 million per year, certainly a large agency — and yet no-one ever referred to me as a bureaucrat. In moving to another large system, this one in the public sector, how exactly do I metamorphize into a bureaucrat? I assume, frankly, that the word is used so as to prejudice, but between us, I see my mission here as being to de-bureaucratize the system. It's a little point, I know, but I always try very hard not to depersonalize.

Well, those are my thoughts. This has run on longer than I intended. I'm on vacation through February 18, but give me a call after that if you want to discuss any of them. Stay well.
Sincerely,

Will

Will Lightbourne
Administrator

So you can see from this very careful and painstaking letter how complicated the problem is beyond my superficial point of view. I have never been to the General Assistance office. I don't know what goes on there. I have to correct my understanding of what we talked about over coffee by what is stated in the letter. I never called him a bureaucrat. He is the opposite of an apparatchik, as demonstrated by the efforts he has made since assuming the job. But there is something massively wrong with the system and it needs overhauling in a radical way. Will Lightbourne, to me, represents someone you can work with in a cooperative way to effect the changes that are needed. I am grateful for his response.

In a way, the impression I had of the Welfare System is rather like my first impression of the homeless. I was caught in a circumstance where I was observing my own response rather than critically appraising a system I knew very little about. Therefore, I was dealing with predispositions rather than the reality of the matter. Predispositions are something you hopefully grow out of as you learn from experience. I still have a lot to learn.

The following is the *"Mission Statement"* of the Human Resources Agency:

> The Human Resources Agency of Santa Cruz County serves those among us who suffer hardship: the poor, the vulnerable, and the exploited in our community. We assist in many ways—with income and direct benefits to help meet daily needs; with employment training and placement services to enable economic self-sufficiency; with protective services to shield against abuse; and with social services to help each individual develop their fullest human potential.
>
> With the public as a whole, we work to develop a socially and economically healthy community. We serve as conveners and supporters of the wider human services movement, and as facilitators of economic vitality to ensure that there will be productive opportunities for all to participate in.
>
> We are motivated by the recognition that each person we assist is an individual with worth and dignity. The services we provide are theirs by human right. Each client is treated with absolute courtesy and compassion, and is empowered by being involved, to the greatest extent possible, in the decisions that will affect his or her life. We succeed in our mission to the extent that the people we serve are prepared and supported to meet the challenge of their lives with a greater measure of hope.

As the staff of HRA, we emphasize team-work, a
spirit of "si se puede", and a commitment to mutual
respect and support of each other's dignity. We
emphasize shared involvement in decision-making,
and the responsible delegation of authority to the
levels where key tasks are implemented. The most
important role in our agency is service to our clients,
and all support and management functions are committed to assist staff to perform direct services. The
County developed two position papers on the homeless in 1991. They provided an inventory of services
currently available to homeless people in the county
and an assessment of major remaining service gaps.
In the first paper, the conclusion reached was that
many services were being provided; the second paper
addressed the remaining needs to be met.

The inadequate services identified were: case management and service
coordination. This is the big question. The costs far outrun the delivery.
Case-management is the name of the problem not the solution, if we are
to listen to Tillich about what it means to be turned into an object to be
managed, even if it is unavoidable. Of course, it is the necessary condition of social welfare efforts, but who wants to suffer it? For this reason,
people in need often avoid the system and look elsewhere for help or
despair of finding any. Better to visit every church in the community and
look for someone who might help than go to the Human Resources
Agency and apply for General Assistance. Better to scrounge in dempster
dumpsters. Not one remark is made about the General Assistance program in the County Briefing Paper. They do not even take into account
what is wrong in their own system in their effort to address the problem.
Obviously, it is easier to begin new programs than overhaul existing ones.

The report does recognize the need for a nonprofit implementation of
the case management need. This is construed as a "Homeless Case
Management Center." Just the choice of words to be avoided at all costs
although the nonprofit aspect in terms of management is wise. It is the
main point of the recent report developed by the Mayor of New York's

commission on the homeless. City run shelter programs are an acknowl-
edged failure. Nonprofits can do it better and cheaper.

"As envisioned by the Human Resource Administration staff, the HCMC
would be implemented by a private nonprofit agency and funded by a
combination of private and public sources. We estimate the program's
first-year budget at $315,000." The program would be funded from pri-
vate funds, outside of the County Budget, with some token funds provided by the County. There is no mention made that the program could be
funded and staffed by the General Assistance Program.

The bias against single males is indicated when it is clear that the program would be aimed at 120 families rather than single males. It shows
how complicated the situation is, or, how simple. It is a matter of figures.
Work out your budget for 120 families. Divided into $315,000.
Formally, it sounds like taking the GA Budget and moving it to AFDC.

Without prejudging it, figure it out. What is $315,000 divided by 120.
Figure $3,000 a family. It is cheap at twice the price. In order to amelio-
rate the case management stigma, and the worry about being objectified,
the entrepreneur concept could be introduced. The $3,000 is broken up
into $1,000 loans and cottage industries are introduced with the appropri-
ate training. The market will take care of the industry. But none of this
is considered within the context of "case management".

According to the report many homeless people are unable to make a
direct transition from the streets or emergency shelter to permanent
housing. Transitional housing is defined as subsidized housing in which
clients may stay for 6 to 18 months, while paying rent and participating in
programs toward self-sufficiency. To qualify for transitional housing,
clients must have achieved a fairly high level of functioning, which, given
their homelessness, is contradictory. What are we talking about? Former
computer programmers temporarily out of work?

We tried this effort. It was a disaster. Well, half disaster, and half not so
bad. We rented a house a few blocks down from the River Street
Shelter. It was home for seven homeless males. It needed regular super-

visorial management which we were not prepared or organized to give, although Paul Pfotenhauer responded to all of the emergencies and did his best to befriend those living there. We got stuck with the rent when someone left in the middle of the month. We had no contingency funds. There was shaky morale in the house. An eccentric guy named Pinky (he always wore pink) annoyed his housemates who periodically beat him up and the police had to be called. Stuff like that. But we managed to carry it for almost two years. It was an experiment that tested our limits. We exceeded them, our limits, that is. Partly because we rented another house. Drug addicts moved in before we had time to fix it up—it was a mess. Before we shut it down we owed the landlord hundreds of dollars he is still trying to collect. We gave up on renting houses without a strong support system.

Conditions are developing for a concerted and organized plan to help the homeless in terms of long-range solutions to the problem. I am aware of my own ambivalence toward official efforts and how long they take to be implemented and at what cost. But the report makes it clear that non-profit agencies are important for implementation; without them, the County is stuck in their own lack of resources, although a cursory glance at the Annual County Budget ($250,000,000.00) demonstrates a wildly distorted sense of priorities beginning with new desks and chairs for practically everyone employed.

In a more recent report—October 16, 1991, the following proposals are put forth:

"*Goal No. One* The private and public sectors should work together to facilitate the provision of case management services for homeless and at-risk families and individuals throughout the county who are ready to take the steps necessary to achieve independence. The services should be closely linked with transitional housing and could be provided by a non-profit agency which operates its own transitional housing, and/or by a social service agency working cooperatively with nonprofit developers who provide and manage transitional housing units. To facilitate the development of countywide case management services, the following actions are being taken or are recommended:

The United Way of Santa Cruz County and the Greater Santa Cruz County Community Foundation have indicated their willingness to participate in developing a plan for providing case management services to homeless and at-risk families and individuals throughout the county, and obtaining support for these services;

The Human Resources Agency will continue to coordinate with the Greater Santa Cruz Community Foundation, United Way of Santa Cruz County, and interested service providers to determine how case management services can best be provided, to identify appropriate agencies to provide these services; to identify potential funding sources; and to develop a detailed design, budget, and implementation plan.

In the event that a new private nonprofit agency is needed, and is created to provide case management services, the United Way of Santa Cruz County has agreed to serve as temporary fiscal agent until the new agency receives its tax-exempt status.

The Human Resources Agency has agreed to provide ongoing technical assistance and consultation regarding both fundraising and program development.

Although it is anticipated that the bulk of the funding for case management services will come from private sources, local governments are encouraged to consider providing support to program operations in partnership with the private sector.

"*Goal No. Two* Local jurisdictions and housing development agencies should work together to facilitate the development of new transitional housing units for homeless families and individuals. A reasonable initial goal is to develop units capable of housing 40 homeless families (35 in North County and five in South County) and 20 single adults. Once these units have been developed and operated for some time, the remaining need should be assessed.

Potential funding sources for transitional housing development include HUD programs administered by the Housing Authority of Santa Cruz County, the HUD McKinney Transitional Housing Program, County and City CDBG funds, County and City Redevelopment Agency funds, and other developmental agencies. In addition, several local nonprofit agencies are currently developing housing projects that could potentially provide a number of transitional housing units.

To facilitate the development of transitional housing, the following actions are being taken or are recommended:

> The Housing Authority of Santa Cruz County, in collaboration with the Human Resources Agency, has recently been awarded HUD McKinney funds to acquire and operate 6 units of transitional housing for homeless families with children in northern Santa Cruz County;

> The County Redevelopment Agency's Board of Directors has authorized a grant of $196,875 from the County Redevelopment Agency's Low and Moderate-Income Housing Fund to assist in acquisition and rehabilitation of a transitional housing facility by the Housing Authority;

> Housing agencies, local Redevelopment Agencies, and social service agencies are encouraged to work together to identify potential sites and funding sources, and to develop an implementation plan to provide new transitional housing units;

> Local community development agencies and non-

profit service providers are encouraged to consider
incorporating transitional housing units into projects
currently being planned or developed; and

Local governments are encouraged to develop mech-
anisms to address the development of transitional
housing in their General Plans.

"Goal No. Three The public and private sectors should work together to
facilitate the development of a day resource center for homeless individuals in the City of Santa Cruz, in order to provide daytime access to sanitary and laundry facilities, storage space for personal items, and a central
location for contact with outreach workers from other service programs.
Funding and support should come from public and private sources.

To facilitate the development of a day resource center, the following
actions are being taken or recommended:

The operators of the highly successful Free Meal
program have announced their intention to develop
and operate the day resource center and have begun
to seek funds for the program;

Housing For Independent People, (HIP), has agreed
to serve as landlord for the day resource center and
is working with the City of Santa Cruz and the Free
Meal Program to purchase and renovate the site;

The office of the City Manager of Santa Cruz and
the County Human Resources Agency are working
with the Free Meal Program to identify potential
federal, state, and private funding cources, and to
develop a detailed program design, budget and
implementation plan;

The City Council of the City of Santa Cruz has set
aside Community Development Block Grant funds

in the amount of $175,000 for homeless facilities and
$45,916 for homeless services, and has identified the
day resource center as a priority for the use of these
funds, pending submission of a final proposal;

The Board of Supervisors of the County of Santa
Cruz has approved the preliminary reservation of
$818,000 in Series C Revenue Bonds proceeds to
assist in the purchase of a facility for the day
resource center, pending development of a mutually
acceptable agreement among the County, the City of
Santa Cruz, and Housing For Independent People;

The Chair of the Board of Supervisors, County
Administrative Officer, City Manager of the City of
Santa Cruz, and Housing For Independent People
are encouraged to continue to work together to
develop a mutually acceptable agreement for the use
of Series C Bonds proceeds to assist in the facility
purchase; and

The Human Resources Agency has agreed to continue providing the day resource center with ongoing
technical assistance and consultation regarding both
fundraising and program development."

The County, therefore, is developing a plan. Administrators were quick to
respond to the need for a Homeless Service Center and it is hoped that one
will open this year (1992). The process hit a snag when a toxic problem was
located in the vicinity of the proposed center. At first it looked like a major
obstacle with thousands of dollars needed to clean up the area as the problem had developed over decades, but the word is that a monitoring device
may be sufficient to respond to the problem which is not as bad as was
thought. Unforeseen problems like that loom up when least expected.

Obviously, daytime access to sanitary and hygiene facilities is a great
need, if you are forced to leave in the morning, in terms of whatever shel-

ter you may have had for the night, and not allowed back until 5:00 p.m., what do you do with yourself in a community that is hostile to the way you look. We couldn't believe it when this condition was imposed on us when we ran the River Street Shelter. We didn't have a daytime use permit. None was offered. The process struck us as insurmountable—public hearings, etc.

The authorities at the time, John Laird and Mardi Wormhoudt, were buckling under pressure from the guy across the street—Rick Santee—and so they stuck it to us. Rumour had it that he had contributed to their campaigns and he was outraged that we had opened a shelter across the street from his business; you know, a personal insult. He had already organized a neighborhood group to keep a previous shelter from locating in the area and he was furious when we were able to procure the facility at River Street from the university. Our landlord for our transitional house some blocks up on River Street had been a part of his original group and then had had a change of heart. He was the soul of cooperation and no matter how difficult things got while we were renting from him, he was willing to work it out. Mr. Santee, however, remained obdurate in his opposition to the shelter.

As mentioned, the lack of a day time use permit meant that everyone had to leave at 8:00 am and not return until 5:00 pm. We had daytime programs ready to develop, cottage industries, classes, volunteers willing to come in and help, but none of this was possible. And then we had to face the constant complaints of the downtown businesses that the homeless were on the streets and bothering customers. What do you expect if they have no where to go during the day?

It was part of the same set of complications imposed by the officials, in this case, John Laird, where we could not pick up people for our Interfaith Satellite Program in the large protected area behind the shelter, a condition so ludicrous we had to live with it for a year just to teach us a lesson. We had to have a permit and he wouldn't issue it. He said it would have a negative impact on the community, which, of course, meant Mr. Santee. Sometimes, when the issue is so patently absurd, you just live with it, like the pet rats at Cedar Street. The energy and the latitude of action is lacking to overcome it. A certain residue of bitterness remains, often for years after, some of it aimed at yourself for not having the means to overcome the obstacles, namely the obtuse bureaucrat or official in your way.

We complained to Mr. Laird, who was the Mayor at the time and he finally worked out a compromise. Instead of picking up the homeless at the River Street Shelter to take them to churches, they would walk another five blocks into the neighborhood, to the municipal bus garage and we could pick them up there. What sense did that make? So much for the impact on the community. We just went ahead and did it.

There was a point before this where the pickup van had to cruise around downtown for homeless to flag it down to get on to go to a church. Can you imagine the absurdity of it? When we complained that the homeless had to stand in the rain at the bus barn, there being no shelter, Mardi Wormhoudt had to come and take a look thinking that the small over-hang at the top of the wall might be sufficient. It was three feet wide and forty feet high.

When we argued for a cover at the River Street pickup site, once it was clear that this was the obvious place for people to gather, she said we couldn't have a tent because it had to be open to public scrutiny. Only a canopy was acceptable. I laughed out loud. She said it wasn't funny. I said yeah that was the problem. She was worried about what the home-less would do in a tent.

Working with the homeless has made me wonder when perestroika will come to Santa Cruz. When will we be able to purge the equivalents of the bolsheviks, the apparatchiks, ensconced in power in our local govern-mental agencies? Russia can exchange democracy for communism. Democracy is what we have got. We're stuck with it in terms of the cur-rent forms of organization. The City Council, the Board of Supervisors, as forms of government, strike me as inefficient and insufficient, as a sys-tem of political organization, at least when reviewed from the bottom up, from the lowest rung of the welfare system. I consider it intolerable that so much unrelieved suffering is allowed in a community such as ours.

What a dream to dismantle the system and start over from scratch, just to have a breather. Our so-called democratic institutions are in need of reform, beginning with the welfare system.

I still remember my first response to City Council meetings—I thought they had been given their scenario by some devotee of the theatre of the absurd. It was one long rehearsal for "Waiting For Godot". The intimidating atmosphere of approaching a kind of fence and talking through a microphone to other citizens a few feet away just like yourself but who are elevated above you, ensconced in their leather swivel chairs, and looking at you as though you were some further annoyance they have to put up with. They look like high school students sitting around a table in the (non)presence of their principal (the city staff), trying to play at politics and not knowing how. They have received no training for it and they are ill prepared for the moves. They are mostly window dressing for the infra-structures.

At least I discovered one specific law of political action—you can call it "Lee's Law". To get something passed you need the sound of twenty people standing up which is better than one hand clapping when it comes to getting something enacted or at least to get the attention of the elected officials. At the appropriate moment, you turn to the audience from your place at the podium and microphone, after you have made your brief spiel and in a loud and commanding voice, you say: "Would everyone in favor of this proposal, please stand and indicate your support." At that point you want at least twenty people to stand up. The sound they make is what counts! One hundred people would be ideal. It is the sound of the people standing, that peculiar whoosh, and then sitting down, another kind of whoosh, more like a rustle. It is the sound of voters standing up to be counted. You could even record it and play it in lieu of warm bodies and it would have almost the same effect. It's all you need to make them take notice—the city officials. The sound does it. All you have to do is make that sound, otherwise known as "Lee's Law". It is democracy in action.

It was insult on injury when a national church group descended on Santa Cruz and began their earthquake relief, shortly after the Loma Prieta

Earthquake (1989) and didn't want to consider the homeless *before* the earthquake. Forget them. They actually made the distinction in our presence between those who were homeless before the earthquake, whom they would not help, and those who were homeless after the earthquake, whom they were prepared to help, especially those who had homes before the earthquake, the propertied ones, the real Christians. It was an odd application of double predestination, the ultimate theological application of triage, those who were to be saved and those who were left to be damned. I was appalled. I was depressed at the matter-of-fact application of the principle of triage.

Triage had become the key word for my involvement with the homeless. It was the word I had to learn. I went to a County Review of Alcoholism Programs one evening. I wanted to know what was being done for alcoholics. I was to learn that teen-age alcoholism was the big concern, taking precedence over homeless drunks. My homeless drunks, left on the sidewalk at our pickup point (the Loudon Nelson Center, at the time) for the Interfaith Satellite Shelter, would have to pick themselves up in the morning, or whenever they woke up, if they weren't dead, and figure out the next day for themselves.

I worried about them; these dead drunk guys, lying out there on the grass, or sidewalk, abandoned to the elements. What was going to happen to them? They had no where to go and they had no shelter against the night and they were dead drunk, so we couldn't take them to the churches scheduled for the evening. We promised to bring homeless who were not drunk and who were not on drugs. We had to screen them. It was our own self-imposed rule, in order to make the program work, to maintain order. I had a word in my mind when I looked at the drunks we had to leave behind, but I didn't know what the word was. I went to the lecture to find the word.

It came up rather early in the talk. As soon as the speaker used it, I knew it was the word I was looking for, although, to tell you the truth, I didn't really want to find it. It is a disheartening word, a demoralizing word, a tragic word. Everyone who has been to Vietnam knows the word: "triage" is the word. I knew it as soon as I heard it, even though, at the time, I didn't know what it meant. The speaker used it with a sense of familiarity as if everyone knew it and used it. It stuck out in my mind like a sore thumb. I went home with it in mind and I looked it up in the dictionary.

Triage:
A system designed to produce the greatest
benefit from limited treatment facilities for
battlefield casualties
1. *by giving full treatment to those who may survive*
2. *and not to those who have no chance of survival*
3. *and those who will survive without it.*

A system used to allocate a scarce commodity,
such as food or housing, only to those capable
of deriving the greatest benefit from it.

French. < trier, to sort

Isn't that terrific! It is a rationalization for giving up or not even making the effort. No question about it. There are a number of fallacies operating to make the rationalization appear logical. The first analogy is with warfare—the first fallacy. It is the worst possible situation applied to peace-time. We are not at war. And yet war is the model for applying triage to the homeless. In fact, the homeless male is the targeted victim. He is the object of triage: no chance of survival. Don't even go near him. No wonder the homeless Vietnam vet makes up a significant part of this group.

Next fallacy: limited treatment facilities. The commodities, the resources, are not scarce; they are in wasteful abundance. Take a horrendous storm. Mud slides. People evacuated from their homes. Shelters are available, with beds, blankets, pillows, hot coffee, t.v., and food, within 8 hours or less, for as many as there are rendered homeless. No triage practised there. The resources are inexhaustible when they want to be. But you had best be a homeowner before you become homeless to have them available to you.

114

When you see an African-American and a Latin-American lying drunk on the lawn or the sidewalk try to find the resources then. It is applied triage. 50% of homeless men, nationally, are black or Latino.

Take the principle of triage up a level and apply it to the organization of the social welfare system. One third of the system is inoperable and where one withholds scant and scarce resources, remember the phrase— "limited treatment facilities"—there you find the practice of triage at the institutional structural level. General Assistance is our version of institutionalized triage, although the situation is not as grim as I first thought. Reforms have been made even though the system itself is in need of reform. It costs $200,000 to give the money to the triaged victims of our social system of welfare.

I became obsessed with the word. I wondered: does God practice triage? It was the one thing I thought God wouldn't do. Not my God. God is no respecter of persons. God does not do triage. In fact, the rejected third, according to another meaning of the word, in French, are just those God cares most about. God does *reverse* triage. God makes them the object of salvation. Like Jesus said: "The last will be first."

This was the biblical teaching on the homeless. They really were the favored of God. The victims are the ones God goes after. The last will be first. Blessed are the homeless for they will enter into the many mansions where a place has been prepared for them.

This view of the homeless is unacceptable because it is the Gospel; it is a paradox; it contradicts conventional wisdom; it is foolishness to the Greeks and even worse to the residents of Santa Cruz. But the message is getting across: we are too susceptible to the ironic notion, *reversing the above*, that there, but for the grace of God, go you and I, and we find resources among us to reach out and help those in need. The work has just begun. I hope to see the problem of homelessness in Santa Cruz solved in my lifetime.

What's wrong with tents? What's wrong with yurts? What's wrong with cheap, low-cost, buildings, like log cabins? What's wrong with garden cottages?

It is impossible to put up a donated mobile home for the homeless in Santa Cruz County. I can show you the letter I got from the County CAO, formerly the head of HRA. She said it would cost over $30,000 and you would have to get permits to open a mobile home park. I didn't want to get a two page letter on why I can't hook up a donated mobile home. Obviously, it died there.

The obstacles are transparent and the people who man the barricades to see to it that people in need are not given shelter are in power. They need to be replaced before a solution can be found. I bear a grudge against them. They were not willing to cooperate then and there is little reason to believe they will cooperate now. *They have to be forced to comply.* We need a set of resolutions to implement against the bureaucrats who stand in the way of solving this problem. *They must be forced to comply.*

See what I mean about old grievances dying hard. Actually, the situation has changed dramatically in the last half decade. Much progress has been made. The tide turned when Don Lane was elected to the Santa Cruz City Council. He ran on a platform pledging his concern for the homeless. He has done much to fulfill that pledge. It has to do with making oneself available. When Mardi Warmhoudt was Mayor her official stand was to refer to the Federal Government—*they* had to do something, not her. It wasn't a local problem, she argued, a pretty dumb argument when you look at the local homeless. She was devoid of ideas and admitted as much, which hardly needed stating. Don Lane changed all that. He brought up the camping ban for discussion at a City Council meeting. They stared him down. Nobody said a word. It was like walking past someone in need in order to get home for the evening news and a martini. It was both the worst moment in City Government and the turning point. Now Don Lane is the Mayor of Santa Cruz.

Then came Katherine Beiers, who has been the chief advocate of the Homeless Garden Project, and Scott Kennedy, who is willing to help in every way, with his unfailing sympathy for the underdog. Suddenly, a new political climate, in support of programs for the homeless, had emerged in Santa Cruz.

Mention should be made of the S.S.I. Program run by the State. If you are mentally disturbed and cannot function in any kind of normal job environment, if you are disabled and cannot work, you can apply for what is called S.S.I. (Supplemental Security Income). You receive a monthly check and you become a permanent welfare client, supported for the rest of your life. I remembered how LSD casualties, those who never recovered from their acid trips in the 1960s, and therefore would never have a normal life, applied for S.S.I. and were supported with a monthly stipend. The problem with applying now is that you are routinely denied. *Everyone* who applies is denied, as a matter of course. What the hell kind of a welfare program is that? Then you have to appeal. Usually, the appeal is denied. Then you have recourse to appeal again and often the third appeal is granted. If not, you can take it to court, where, sometimes, you may be granted S.S.I, by the judge. One of the difficulties with this routine is that people end up with a large "retro" check, often many thousands of dollars, accumulated from the months of appeals. The windfall brings with it more problems than the monthly check for people unused to handling money. In a way, it is worse than General Assistance on the County level, so skewed is the welfare system in this country.

The homeless, of course, are at the bottom of the barrel in terms of eligibility for social services. It brings one to a theory about the homeless we have as yet to develop. Triage was bad enough, but it did not give rise to a theory. It only accounted for the argument in behalf of scarce resources, what was the phrase—"limited treatment facilities"! It did not account for the attitude toward the homeless without a war to justify that attitude in the application of triage.

My wife warns me about being pedantic. Well, here it comes.

The theory about homelessness I have recourse to is about victimage. It has been developed by Jacques Derrida and Rene Girard. Derrida writes about it in terms of the scapegoat ritual of ancient Greece and Girard develops it into a full blown theory about the sacred. According to Girard, it is a theory of religion because he makes an equation between violence and the sacred. It has a certain relentless logic if you take the crucified Jesus as the reference point.

I will only repeat a number of points here and the reader will have to repair to the texts in question for the full discussion:

Jacques Derrida: *Disseminations*, Chapter 1, "Plato's Pharmacy", University of Chicago Press, Rene Girard: *Things Hidden From the Foundation of the World*, Stanford University Press, 1987

Derrida refers to the old ritual of Ancient Greece, the 6th Day of Thargelion, in the Greek calendar, an annual event, when two men, (they could have been homeless), saved for the occasion, and fed well, are taken to the outermost precincts of the city, on the day of the festival, and there, after they are beaten on their genitals with leeks, are murdered and burned, "in order to rid the city of pollution". Old rituals die hard. These men are the homeless in our midst and I am ready to believe that vigilante posses in our community could still be summoned to take their unfortunate victims out to be burned, in the spirit of the old Greek festival. To rid the city of pollution.

It was called the Festival of the *Pharmakon*. It was a variant of the "wounded healer". They were a medicine, a drug, a remedy, for the ills of the city. They were the scapegoats, one of the *meanings* of *pharmakon*. Poisons in proper doses are medicines, according to the appropriate ritual.

> "Tzetzes gives the following account, based on certain frag-
> ments by the satirical poet Hipponax, of the ceremony:
> "The (rite of the) pharmakos was a purification of this sort
> of old. If a calamity overtook the city by the wrath of God,
> whether it were famine or pestilence or any other mischief,
> they led forth as though to a sacrifice the most unsightly of
> them all as a purification and a remedy to the suffering
> city. They set the sacrifice in the appointed place, and gave
> him cheese with their hands and a barley cake and figs, and
> seven times they smote him with leeks and wild figs and
> other wild plants. Finally they burnt him with fire with the
> wood of wild trees and scattered the ashes into the sea and to
> the winds, for a purification, as I said, of the suffering city."
> Derrida, *Disseminations*, p. 133.

118

Walter Burkert, in his *Greek Religion*, makes this comment after his discussion of the Pharmakos ritual:

> *"To expel a trouble-maker is an elementary group reflex; perhaps in the most distant background there is also the situation of the pack surrounded by beasts of prey: only if one member, preferably a marginal, weak, or sick member, falls victim to the beasts can the others escape. The outcast is then also the saviour to whom all are most deeply indebted."* (p.84)

The scapegoat ritual was also enacted in Israel as in the so-called mocking of Jesus, in a ritual known as the "Cabbage-King", where the victim is dressed as a King, given a crown of thorns, and run through the gauntlet of Roman soldiers, mocked, beaten, and finally crucified. And the phrase from the above quote—"the most unsightly of them all"—is an echo of Isaiah regarding his prophecy of the coming Messiah who would be a leper and therefore the ugliest of them all.

Girard develops this victimization ritual into a full-blown theory. You have to read it and re-read it and then re-read it again. He is even more dense than Derrida which is some distinction. It takes unusual effort to absorb the argument. But the insights are there, with ample borrowing from Freud.

I am at a loss to summarize it here in reference to the homeless; the scapegoat theme and the theme of victimization are all we need to mention, obvious enough in themselves, as a means of interpreting the plight of the homeless and the role they play in their rejection by the community.

I don't want to be a victim anymore than you do. I don't want to become homeless. I don't want to be abandoned to the streets and then arrested for wanting a place to lie down for the night with or without a blanket. I don't want to lurk in doorways. I don't want to panhandle and then be arrested for that. I don't want to be found by the police and beaten. I don't want to be murdered and thrown into the San Lorenzo River. I don't want to be pushed off a bridge in San Lorenzo Park. I don't want to be arrested for urinating in public when I have no place to go but in my pants. I don't want to be abandoned to dread and despair and the anxiety of emptiness and meaninglessness—with my only relief in drugs and alcohol.

One could ask: why don't more homeless people commit suicide? We have Mitch Snyder to think about as one who did just that, reduced to self-destruction, self-victimized, hanging himself in his room in the huge homeless shelter he organized in Washington, D. C.

After I recovered from my first impression of the homeless as members of Dante's Hell, and after we opened the Cedar Street Shelter, I got over my sense of their despair and despondency, watching all the guys get up in the morning, I was amazed at how basically cheerful and full of vitality many of them were. I was reminded of the saying of the early Greek philosopher—Heraclitus: "The sun is new every day." I had the sense it was life-itself, manifest life, expressing itself, in and through them, in spite of their abject situation. And, after all, many of them were young and full of beans.

But the question of suicide as the end of despair still comes to mind. Isn't homelessness the final index of the human predicament, the boundary line beyond which one cannot go? No, homelessness is not this state itself, unless, in the situation of homelessness, one falls into despair, something not all homeless do. Homelessness is not the *end of possibilities.* In fact, we see it now as a whole new context for possibilities, a challenge for anyone to address. But, in despair, a person *has* come to the end of his or her possibilities.

As Tillich writes in his *Systematic Theology, II*, in the section on "Despair and the problem of suicide":

"The word itself means "without hope" and expresses the feeling of a situation from which there is 'no exit' (Sartre). The most impressive description of the situation of despair has been given by Kierkegaard in *Sickness Unto Death*, where 'death' means beyond possible healing."

"Despair is the state of inescapable conflict. It is the conflict, on the one hand, between what one potentially is and therefore ought to be and, on the other hand, what one actually is in the combination of freedom and destiny. The pain of despair is the agony of being responsible for the loss of the meaning of one's existence and of being unable to recover it. One is shut up in one's self and in the conflict with one's self. One cannot escape, because one cannot escape from one's self. It is out of this situation that the question arises whether suicide may be a way of getting rid of one's self."

Tillich goes on to mention a suicidal tendency in life generally, "the longing for rest without conflict. The human desire for intoxication is a consequence of this longing."

This certainly explains the prevalence of alcoholism among the homeless, as well as those who have homes.

Why did Mitch commit suicide? Was it the penalty he had to pay for his commitment to nonviolence and his following Gandhi? Gandhi states that *satyagraha*, which is what he called his movement of nonviolence, is the willingness to *pay the penalty* for noncompliance with evil. Gandhian nonviolence is a curious decision to be self-victimized in the willingness to pay the penalty for the refusal to cooperate with evil. Mitch got caught in this snare. His resistance to the evil of homelessness, for which he was willing to pay the penalty, probably more than anyone else in the country, this resistance, wore him out and he succumbed to non-resistance to threatening annihilation: his unconscious will to live was undermined.

> *"In every moment of intolerable, insuperable, and mean-ingless pain there is the desire to escape the pain by getting rid of one's self."*
> Tillich, p. 75f.

We had to witness a suicide upon my return from a summer in Wisconsin in the Fall of l991. One of the workers in our garden had been fired; days later, he threw himself in front of a truck on the freeway adjacent to the River Street Shelter. Everyone around him knew he was going to do it.

His name was Dave McGall. He was twenty-seven.

We had a memorial service for him in the garden.

The garden is our place of refuge from such blows. Gardens have always symbolized a place apart from the conflicts of the world, a place to withdraw to where one can be refreshed and enjoy the pleasures that gardening brings. Nothing restores the spirit like gardening.

It is in the garden that the homeless find a home, a place to work, a place to be productive, a place to observe the principle of plenitude thanks to the bounty of the earth—an ethic of abundance. Gardens have always been a harbinger, as well as a memory, of paradise. Paradise is a Persian word meaning a walled place, closed off from the worries of the world, which is why gardens are often enclosed by a wall. Gardens are a place of affirmation for which Eden and Arcadia are the ultimate symbols. It is in the Garden that the affirmation of the unambiguous goodness of creation is made, a defense against everything that would conspire to undo us and defeat us.

The garden, more than anything, establishes a sense of place. It is the best antidote to homelessness.

> The "garden" is the place where the curse upon the land is overcome. In it vegetable nature is liberated from chaos and self-destruction; "weed" there is none. This "garden of the gods," of which every human garden is a symbol and an anticipation, will reappear in the salvation of nature.
>
> Paul Tillich: *The Meaning of Health*

Appendix 1: Remembering Mitch Snyder

*"Remember Mitch Snyder", by Marcia A. Timmel,
reprinted, with permission, from the The Catholic
Worker, Dec. 1990, p.7.*

"In May of 1981 I moved to Washington, D.C., to live and work with the Community for Creative Nonviolence on their "Call to Prayer and Resistance," a month-long campaign challenging the Reagan administration's policies of militarism at the expense of social programs. It was then that I first got to know Mitch Snyder. To tell the truth, Mitch and I didn't get along with each other all that well. "He is arrogant, dominating, demanding, and he uses people," I often said, "and those are his good qualities!" Which of course in many ways they were, for in Mitch (as in all of us) those traits which were his greatest strengths were also his greatest weaknesses.

Mitch was absolutely clear in his vision of justice for the poor, which translated into a certainty he was right when he spoke and acted on their behalf. Arrogant, yes, but an arrogance rooted in the conviction that Jesus meant exactly what He said when He told us to shelter the homeless and feed the hungry, and give all we have to the poor. Anything less was compromising the Gospel.

This certainty gave Mitch a compelling quality. When he spoke to an issue in a group he spoke with an instant authority. In a community of equals, he was dominant, sometimes through charisma and sometimes through the sheer forcefulness of his vision. Mitch possessed a prophetic tenacity that often seemed to overwhelm even those very friends who wanted to work with him. Like a brilliant flame, he illuminated, yet at once consumed the atmosphere around him, so that those who tried to share his light often found themselves trapped like moths in his aura.

Mitch was demanding. Seven-day weeks were his norm, and he expected no less of those he worked with. How could we give less, when all around us the Body of Christ was dying in the person of the poor? There was an urgency in Mitch that was never satisfied. This driven character in the end drove countless people away from community with Mitch; some (those who tried to meet his demands) into burnout, some into the cynical decision that helping the poor just wasn't worth the bother, and even more (like myself) into other communities where we continue to struggle with the questions Mitch confronted us with. For Mitch was right: We are not doing enough. Yet somehow we have to come to terms with that inadequacy, confess it humbly before God, and find some way to continue our meager efforts through the long haul.

Undergirding all this blessed hubris was his love — a fierce love, and often angry love. Over the years, Mitch's motives were often questioned by many who chose not to love (or were unable to love) so intensely. Particularly during the 80's, as Mitch became a "success" in his cause, drawing national attention to the scandal of homelessness in this country, he was accused of being an "egotist" whose tactics were simply a form of grandstanding. The possibility that a man could love so passionately as to repeatedly risk his life through starvation while he fasted or through exposure as he chose to spend winters on the grates of Washington's streets, or to endure the stress of ongoing confrontations with power and the harassment of arrest and trial, were simply incomprehensable to the "me generation." And so Mitch was alternately lauded as a saint or castigated as a fraud. He was neither. He was simply a man who loved Jesus, and who loved the poor because Jesus told him he should. Love endures what ego cannot.

The Logic of Love

It was because of this love that many of us who usually didn't get along with Mitch so well continued to work with him over the years. Even when he was being arrogant and dominating, even when you felt he might be using you, you just couldn't escape the compelling logic of his love. He might be a pain, but he was usually right.

Because of Mitch's love (and a few sit-ins and a dramatic Congressional feast prepared from dumpstered foods), food that grocers and caterers used to destroy each day in dumpsters is now distributed to the hungry through food banks and community agencies. Because of Mitch's love (and a grueling summer fast in Kansas) food that the government used to let rot in caves below the ground in the name of "supporting agriculture" now feeds the hungry from soup kitchens and food pantries around the country. Because of Mitch's love (and a winter encampment called "Reaganville" in Lafayette Park, and numerous fasts, and ongoing campaigns of civil disobedience) the dozens who used to freeze to death on Washington's streets each winter now find shelter at the model Federal City Shelter run by CCNV, and for six years have found legal shelter under the provisions of Initiative 17, which guaranteed every person's right to clean and decent shelter.

The homeless are sheltered, the hungry are fed, the naked are clothed, the thirsty are given drink, the sick are cared for, prisoners are joined, and the homeless dead are claimed and cremated. Mitch neglected none of the corporal works of mercy, and in the process he also embodied the spiritual works of mercy: he counseled those of us who were doubtful, instructed the ignorant, comforted the afflicted, admonished fools and sinners, forgave those who abused him, prayed for the dead, and in the words of Mother Jones, "worked like hell for the living."

During the last six months of his life Mitch showed me a side of himself I had never experienced before. One conversation in particular, at the Plowshares sentencing in Norristown, PA in April, introduced me to that side of him that was vulnerable, that shared some of the same hopes and fears of every human being. He was tired and demoralized that in recent months there had appeared a growing backlash against the homeless. They were no longer a "chic" social issue the media had decreed, and since they had the temerity to be with us (as Jesus had promised) even after a few programs had been thrown their way, there was a growing resentment towards them in our culture which prides itself on "eliminating problems." Mitch felt this all as a crushing personal responsibility. He spoke of his own hunger, of his disappointment at missing out on a month-long retreat that he had hoped to take. Yet even in the midst of all this personal disappointment he took the time to discuss with me how my pregnancy was going and how my little three-year-old was doing. It was almost as if children were speaking to him of fresh promise. I found myself realizing that not only did I respect and admire Mitch (which I always had, even when he was being his most irascible) I actually liked him.

Appendix 2: The Philosophy of Social Work
Paul Tillich

We include the following address by Paul Tillich on the philosophy of social work as a basis for discussing the meaning of homelessness in Santa Cruz. Tillich defines some of the main principles of working with anyone in need, the object of social welfare, e.g., the homeless. His brief discussion is one of the best statements of a philosophy of social work.

> *The Philosophy of Social Work*
> by Paul Tillich
>
> *[Privately circulated in pamphlet form and then published
> in The Social Service Review (Chicago). vol. 36 no. 1,
> 1962, p. 13—16. and In German: "Ethische Grundsatze
> der sozialen Arbeit," Gessamelte Werke XIII. p. 221-26.]*

The following excerpts are from a talk given by Paul Tillich, on November 12, 1961, the occasion of the 25th Anniversary of *Selfhelp*, Inc., a nonprofit social service group aiding refugees, who had fled Hitler's Germany, to settle in the United States. Tillich was the Honorary Chairman of the group.

The basis of all social work is the deficiency of every legal organization of society. A perfectly functioning organization of the whole society, a social mechanism embracing all mankind would not leave room for social work, but such a mechanism is unimaginable. It is prevented by two factors, one of which is rooted in what we call today in philosophical jargon "our existential predicament", our insufficiency. The second factor is rooted in our existential nature, the uniqueness of every individual and every situation. No total regulation, even if given in the best interest of everybody, ever has adequately functioned either in war or in peace. The disorder produced by totalitarian regulations in Nazi Germany during the Second World War is equaled by the disorder in food distribution in Soviet Russia during the present cold war. Neither intellect nor charac-

ter of men or women are adequate to such a task.   And even if they were
in one part of the world, interferences from other parts would spoil the
functioning of a perfect social organization. The fact on which *Selfhelp* is
based, the European immigration, was for a long time beyond the reach
of any existing legal organization of social needs. Spontaneous social
work was the only way to solve the immediate problem.

But this is a minor part of our question. More important is the fact that
even in the best legal organization of social needs, every individual represents a unique problem. Only in a society which suppresses individual
claims for help can this problem be put aside, and not only individual persons but also individual situations between persons, or persons and
groups, transcend the reach of any legal organization. It is the greatness
of human beings that their freedom implies a uniqueness which prohibits
being absorbed into a social machine so long as they remain human. For
this reason social work is more than emergency work, unless one defines
emergency as a perpetual concomitant of the human situation—and that
probably is true.

Certainly all social work tries to make itself superfluous and many forms
of it have done so. And in all our discussions we often have asked ourselves whether we have already reached that stage, but each time we
found a large amount of emergency situations which required the contin-
uation of our way of social work.

We tried to listen to the situation as we did in the years of our foundation, and in doing so we tried one of the great laws of life, the law of "listening love". It is one of the decisive characteristics of love that it listens
sensitively and reacts spontaneously. As one of our early friends, Max
Wertheimer, has indicated, situations have a voiceless voice. "Things
cry", he used to say, but also what cries most intensively are situations.

It was the cry of a particular situation which we hardly could have
ignored and which drove us to found *Selfhelp*. And it was not only the
beginning of our history in which this happened. Again and again we
had to listen sensitively and to react spontaneously. It is certain that in
some situations we were not sensitive enough and reacted not sponta-

neously enough, but it was a fundamental principle of our philosophy of social work.

Social work is centered in individuals. The most concrete, and therefore most important, representative of social work is the case-worker, and what is valid for the case-worker is valid for the whole organization in relation to the individual. The case-worker also must listen sensitively and respond spontaneously. The case-worker meets the individual and is in the understandable temptation of transforming care into control. The case-worker is in danger of imposing instead of listening, and acting mechanically instead of acting spontaneously. Every social worker knows this danger, but does not always notice succumbing to this temptation. The case-worker should not make a harsh judgment about it, but from time to time should restate the principle of "listening love" in order to dissolve any hardening mechanism in those who do social work.

The danger of which I am speaking is a tendency in every dealing with other persons to treat them as objects, as things to be directed and managed. It was always a symbol for me that the patients of the social worker were called cases. I do not know whether a better word can be found but the word "case" automatically makes of the individual an example for something general. Who, I ask all of you, wants to be a case, but we all are cases for the doctor, the counselor, the lawyer, and certainly the social worker. The case-worker is not to be blamed for this inescapable situation but would be blamed if in dealing with the patient, with this case, makes the patient into an object for whom everything is determined and in whom spontaneity is suppressed. The question is whether the case-worker is able to see in the patient not only what is comparable with other cases or identical with what has been experienced with other patients, but that the caseworker sees the incomparable, the unique, rooted in the freedom of the patient. It is the amount of love between the social worker and the patient which here is decisive—the listening, responding, transforming love.

Here, when I use the term love, as before, I certainly do not mean the love which is emotion; nor do I think of *philia*—of friendship which only really develops between the social worker and the patient, nor do I think of the love which is *Eros*, which creates an emotional desire towards the patient that in many cases is more destructive than creative; rather, it is the love whose name in Greek is *agape* and in Latin *caritas*—the love which descends to misery and ugliness and guilt in order to elevate. This love is critical as well as accepting, and it is able to transform what it loves. It is called *caritas* in Latin, but it should not be confused with what the English form of the same word indicates today—namely, charity, a word which belongs to the many words which have a disintegrated, distorted meaning. Charity is often identical with social work, but the word charity has the connotation of giving for good causes in order to escape the demand of love. Charity as escape from love is the caricature and distortion of social work.

Critical love, which at the same time accepts and transforms, needs knowledge of who is the object of love. The social worker must know the patient. But there are two different ways of knowing. We may distinguish them as our knowledge of the other one as a thing, and our knowledge of the other one as a person. The first is the cognition of external facts about somebody. The second is the participation in their inner self—as far as any human being is able to participate in another one. The first is done in detachment, through an empirical approach; the second is done through participation in the inner self of the other one. The first is unavoidable, but never enough in human relations. The second gives the real knowledge, but it is a gift given alone to the intuition of love. Here the social worker is in the situation of all of us in our daily encounters with each other. No amount of factual knowledge about each other can replace the intuition of love, which remains love even if it judges.

This leads to the last and perhaps the most important question—the end, the aim, of social work. The aim has several degrees. The first degree is the conquest of the immediate need, and here the factor of speed is important. The necessity of accepting and being willing to bear the consequences of possible errors, even of helping someone who doesn't deserve help, must be taken by the social worker. It is analogous with love which has the principle that it is better missing several guilty ones than condemning one innocent one. The second degree is the self-abrogation, the self-conquest of social help, as far as possible, by guiding the person into independence. This is attempted always in all social agencies, but we know it is not always possible. Then there is a third stage about which I want to say a few words. On the basis of the present situation as I have seen it in the young people in all the colleges and universities, and in many other people, we mainly need to give the people of our time the feeling of being necessary.

Being necessary is, of course, never absolute. Nobody is indispensable. Nevertheless, somebody who doesn't feel necessary at all, who feels that he or she is a mere burden, is on the edge of total despair. In all groups I found this widespread feeling of not being necessary. There are many reasons for every effect, but one of the reasons for this is that in our secularized society one thing is lost, namely, that, whatever their external destiny may be, people no longer have an eternal orientation, an orientation which is independent of space and time. It is the feeling of having a necessary, incomparable and unique place within the whole of being. Herein lies a danger for uprooted and migrating millions. It is a danger for mankind itself, namely to feel that their existence as a whole is no longer necessary. The easy way in which politically we are playing now with collective suicide is analogous to the phenomenon of individuals who have lost the feeling of a necessary place, not only in their work and community, but also in the universe as a whole.

This leads to a final aim of social work. In helping all individuals to find the place where they can consider themselves as necessary, you help to fulfill the ultimate aim of human beings and their world, namely, the universal community of all beings in which any individual aim is taken into the universal aim of being itself. That is the highest principle of social work and, of course, transcends the limits of its techniques. It is certainly understandable that this aim is not always conscious to those who have the burden of the daily work. But it may help them if they remember it in moments in which they may despair as we all do about the meaning of their work. On the other hand, it may give them a spiritual lift in moments when they feel grateful to hear a response from one of thousands whom we may have helped. It may be of inspiration to us to think that we contribute to the ultimate aim of being itself in our small way— and every individual's way is small. To give such inspiration may be a function of an hour of memory such as the present one.

Bibliography

For the religious background of nonprofit corporations based on the principle of voluntary association, cf. George Hunston Williams: *The Radical Reformation.* Westminster Press, Philadelphia, Pa. 1962. He makes it clear that this principle of voluntary association was born in the sectarian wing of the Protestant Reformation, actually on a given night, when a priest- Joseph Blaurock—was *rebaptized*, thus inaugurating the anabaptist movement. This principle of voluntary association for the freedom of worship (the right to assembly) is the background for the legal form of voluntary associations—the nonprofit corporation. For the sociological and political significance of voluntary associations, cf., the writings of James Luther Adams.

Both men were my professors at Harvard Divinity School.

There are various how-to books on starting and directing a nonprofit corporation.

George Herbert Mead: *Movements of Thought in the 19th Century.* University of Chicago Press, Chicago, 1936. cf. discussion of capitalism and Malthusianism where the increment in population allows for a "starvation wage" as there will always be more people than jobs.

Michael Mollat: *The Poor in the Middle Ages,* Yale University Press, New Haven, 1986, is an excellent historical study. I am grateful to Mark Primack for bringing it to my attention.

Max Weber: *The Protestant Ethic and the Spirit of Capitalism,* Scribners, New York, 1958

The *New Yorker Magazine,* various articles over the past years, the latest on New York shantytowns, July 2, 1991.

M. E. Hombs and Mitch Snyder, *Homelessness in America: A forced march to nowhere,* Community for Creative Non-violence, Washington, D.C., 1982

A. Cibulskis and C. Hoch, *Homelessness: An annotated bibliography,* Council of Planning Librarians, Chicago, 1985

A. L. Schorr, *Common Decency*, Yale U. P., New Haven, Ct., 1986

Belcher and DiBlasio, *Helping the Homeless: where do we go from here?*, Lexington Books, Lexington Ma, 1990

Belcher and Singer, *Homelessness: A cost of capitalism*, Social Policy, 18 (4): 44-48, 1988

E. Burke, *Citizen participation strategies*, Journal of the American Institute of Planners, 34 (5):288, 1968

Burt and Cohen, *America's Homeless: numbers, characteristics and the programs that serve them.* Urban Institute Report 89-3, Washington, 1989.

Carol Caton, *Homeless in America*, Oxford University Press, New York, 1990.

L. Stolarski, Right to Shelter: *History of the Mobilization of the Homeless as a Model of Voluntary Action*, Journal of Voluntary Action Research, 17 (1): 36, 1988

D. Mandelker, et al, *Housing and Community Development*, Bobbs-Merrill, Indianapolis, 1981

Institute of Medicine, *Homelessness, Health, and Human Needs*, National Academy Press, Washington, D.C., 1988.

George Orwell: *Down and Out in Paris and London*, Harcourt Brace, New York, 1933

Peter Rossi, *Down and Out in America: the Origins of Homelessness*, University of Chicago Press, Chicago, 1989.

Block, Cloward, Ehrenreich and Piven, *The Mean Season*, The Attack on the Welfare State, Pantheon Books, New York, 1987

P. Archard, *Vagrancy, Alcoholism and Social Control*, Macmillan, London, 1979

R. Bingham, R. Green and S. White, (eds.), *The Homeless In Contemporary Society*, Sage Publications, Beverly Hills, 1987

M. Dear and J. Wolch, *Landscapes of Despair: From Deinstitutionalization to Homelessness*, Princeton, 1987

Martin Seligman, *Helplessness*, On Depression, Development, and Death, W.H. Freeman, San Francisco, 1975

H. Fingarette, "Alcoholism: The mythical disease." *The Public Interest*, 91: 3-22

Michael Harrington, *The Other America*, Penguin Books, Baltimore, 1963
Decade of Decision, Simon and Schuster, New York, 1980
The New American Poverty, Penguin Books, New York, 1984

Alan Crawford, *Thunder on the Right: The "New Right" and the Politics of Resentment*, Pantheon, New York, 1980

Friedrich Nietzsche, *The Birth of Tragedy and The Geneaology of Morals*, Anchor Books, New York, 1956

Max Scheler, *Ressentiment*, Free Press, 1961

K. Hopper and J. Hamburg, *The Making of America's Homeless: From Skid Row to New Poor, 1945—1984.* Report prepared for the Institute of Social Welfare Research, Community Service Society, New York, 1984.

Thomas Edsall, *The New Politics of Inequality*, Norton, New York, 1984

E. Bassuk, "The homeless problem." *Scientific American*, 251, (1): 40-45, 1986.

Ken Auletta, *The Underclass*, Random House, New York, 1982

James Wright, *Homelessness and Health*, New York, McGraw Hill, 1988.
Address Unknown: The Homeless in America, Aldine de Gruyter, New York, 1989

James Wright, : *"The worthy and unworthy homeless."* Society, 25 (5): 64-69.

Bingham, Green and White, *The Homeless in Contemporary Society*, Sage, Newberry Park, Ca., 1987.

Erickson and Wilhelm, *Housing the Homeless*, Rutgers, New Brunswick, New Jersey, 1986

M. Hope and J. Young, *The Faces of Homelessness*, Heath and Co., Lexington Mass., 1984

Heritage Lectures, *Rethinking Policy on Homelessness*, A conference sponsored by the Heritage Foundation and The American Spectator, Washington, D.C., 1989

Michael Lang, *Homelessness amid affluence: Structure and Paradox in the American Political Economy*, Praeger, New York, 1989.

Levitan and Schillmoeller, *The Paradox of Homelessness in America*, Center for Social Policy, George Washington University, Washington, 1991

National Alliance to End Homelessness, *Housing and Homelessness*, Washington, 1988

R. Sidel, *Women and Children Last: The Plight Of Poor Women In Affluent America*, Penguin, New York, 1986

U.S. General Accounting Office, *Children and Youth.* About 68,000 Homeless and 186,000 In Shared Housing At Any Given Time. GAO/PEMD-89-14, Washington, June, 1989.

Homelessness. Runaway and Homeless Youth Receiving Services at Federally Funded Shelters. GAO/HRD-90-45, Washington, December 1989.

Homelessness. McKinney Act Programs and Funding for Fiscal Year 1989. GAO/RCED-91-126, Washingtion, May 1991

Homelessness. Too Early To Tell What Kinds of Prevention Assistance Work Best. GAO/RCED-90-89, Washington, April 1990

Ruth Ellen Wasem, U.S. Library of Congress. Congressional Research Service. *Homelessness: Issues and Legislation in the 102nd Congress,* Washington, 1988 (Issue brief 88070) Updated regularly.

Edward Klebe, *Homeless Mentally Ill Persons: Problems and Programs,* Washington, 1991, Report No. 91-344 EPW.

Morton Schussheim, *The Cranston-Gonzalez National Affordable Housing Act: Key Provisions and Analysis,* Washington, 1991, Report no. 91-124 RCO.

Susan Vanhorenbeck, *HUD's Shelter Programs For the Homeless,* Washington, 1991, Report no. 91-198 E

Grace Milgram, *Housing: Low and Moderate-Income Assistance Programs,* Washington, Issue brief 91006, Updated regularly.

Morton Schussheim, *Housing: Problems and Policies,* Washington, 1989, Issue brief 89004. Updated regularly.

Ruth Wasem, *Programs Benefiting the Homeless:* FY87-FY89 appropriations trends, Washingtion, 1989, Report no. 89-20 EPW

Carmen Solomon, *Cash Welfare Funds and Homeless Families With Children,* Washington, 1988, Report no. 89-394 EPW

Kirk Nemer, *Homelessness and Commitment: The case of Joyce Brown (a/k/a/ Billie Boggs)* Washingtion, 1988, report no. 88-186 A

R. Goodman, T*he Last Entrepreneurs,* Simon and Schuster, New York, 1979

Doris Lessing: *The Memoirs of a Survivor,* Vintage Books, Random House, New York, 1988, an uncanny and haunting novel projected into the near future anticipating the homeless problem.

Paul Edwards, Editor, "Joseph Popper-Lynkeus", *The Encyclopedia of Philosophy,* MacMillan, New York, 1967

Paul Ricoeur: "The Golden Rule", *New Testament Studies,* 36, 1990, 392-7
The Symbolism of Evil, Harpers, New York, 1967

Paul Tillich: *The Courage To Be,* Yale University Press, New Haven, 1952
Existential Self-Destruction and the Doctrine of Evil, *Systematic Theology,* Vol. II, D. 4.

The Meaning of Despair and Its Symbols, a) Despair and the problem of suicide, pp. 75 ff. University of Chicago Press, 1957.

Paul Lee, *Florence the Goose, A True Story For Children,* The Platonic Academy Press, Santa Cruz, 1992.
Alan Chadwick and the Salvation of Nature, forthcoming, 1992.

John Jeavons: *How To Grow More Vegetables On Less Space,* Ten Speed Press, Berkeley, 1979, available from Ecology Action, 5798 Ridgewood Rd., Willits, Ca. 95490
John Jeavons has done more than anyone to communicate the Chadwick method worldwide. He has a newsletter available from the above address.

Apprenticeships in the Chadwick Method are available at the University of California, Santa Cruz, "Agro-ecology Program", UCSC, Santa Cruz, Ca. 95060.

Richard Merrill: *Radical Agriculture,* Harpers, New York, 1976

Wendell Berry: *The Unsettling of America, Culture and Agriculture,* Sierra Club Press, San Francisco, 1977

Wes Jackson: The Land Institute, Salina, Kansas, is the national center for land reform and sound agricultural practise.

John Prest, *The Garden Of Eden. The Botanic Garden and the Re-Creation of Paradise,* Yale University Press, New Haven, 1981

George Hunston Williams, *Wilderness and Paradise. The Biblical Experience of the Desert in the History of Christianity and the Paradise Theme in the Theological Idea of the University,* Harpers, New York, 1962.

Simone Weil: *The Need For Roots,* Putnam, New York, 1952 is a good place to start. Then read her essay, *The Iliad as a Poem of Force* and apply to the homeless the discussion of the principle of force where a person is turned into a thing or an x. Jack Stauffacher has designed a fine press edition for the Lapis Press, San Francisco, Ca., 1991.

Peter Marin: "The Prejudice Against Men", *The Nation,* July 8, 1991

Nicolas Lemann: *The Promised Land, The Great Black Migration and How It Changed America,* Knopf, New York, 1991, a learned account of the sloganizing effort to help the poor of America which is mostly the history of bureaucratic failure.

David Osborne and Ted Gaebler: *Reinventing Government,* How the Entreprenuerial Spirit Is Transforming the Public Sector, Addison Wesley, Reading Mass., 1992. This should be required reading for everyone in government and everyone aware of and involved in nonprofits.

Jacques Derrida: *Disseminations,* Chapter 1, "Plato's Pharmacy", University of Chicago Press, 1981, is one of the best essays in the history of philosophy and a stunning discussion of the scapegoat theme and the Greek Festival of Thargelion. The punch line is that Socrates was born on the 6th Day of Thargelion, which sealed his fate as the Athenian scapegoat or what Plato called "the truest tragedy".

Rene Girard: *Things Hidden the Foundation of the World*, Stanford U. P., Stanford, 1987 is a running trialogue, on the notion that the sacred is equivalent to violence and victimization, an interesting and complicated thesis on religion as a form of bondage.

Robert Brumbaugh: *The Most Mysterious Manuscript*, University of Southern Illinois Press, Carbondale, 1978 is the best introduction to the Voynich Manuscript problem and failed efforts at its solution or decipherment.

Rudolf Steiner: Various writings on biodynamics, i.e. *Agriculture*, (Lectures). Cf. Anthroposophical Press listings, available from the Biodynamic Farming and Gardening Association,, Box 550, Kimberton, Pa. l9442. Over one hundred titles on Biodynamics are available, e.g., H. H. Koepf: *What is Biodynamic Agriculture?* and Wolf Storl: *Culture and Horticulture, A Philosophy of Gardening*, one of the best introductions to the subject.

Phil Callahan: *Ancient Mysteries, Modern Visions, Acres, USA*, Kansas City, 1984
Callahan's views are given a chapter in *Secrets of the Soil* by Tomkins and Bird, Harpers, New York, 1989

Sigmund Freud: *Collected Papers*: "A Horse Is Being Beaten", Collier Books, New York, 1963

Dostoievsky: *Brothers Karamazov*, Norton, New York, 1976

Footnotes

1. p. xiv The full text of the Shakespeare passage:

> *The quality of mercy is not strain'd,—*
> *It droppeth as the gentle rain from heaven*
> *Upon the places beneath: it is twice blest,—*
> *It blesseth him that gives, and him that takes:*
> *'Tis mightiest in the mightiest: it becomes*
> *The throned monarch better than his crown;*
> *His sceptre shows the force of temporal power,*
> *The atttribute to awe and majesty,*
> *Wherein doth sit the dread and fear of kings;*
> *But mercy is above this sceptered sway,—*
> *It is enthroned in the hearts of kings,*
> *It is an attribute to God himself;*
> *And earthly power doth then show likest God's*
> *When mercy seasons justice.*
> *...................*
> *That, in the course of justice, none of us*
> *Should see salvation: we do pray for mercy;*
> *And that same prayer doth teach us all to render*
> *The deeds of mercy.* p.xiv

This is what Simone Weil meant by learning how to give as if begging. It is the same prayer.

2. p. 3 "Finally, poverty also had a social dimension. In the Middle Ages, to suffer a loss of status meant literally to fall from one's estate, to be deprived of its instruments of labor and of the marks of its condition. For a peasant this meant the loss of farming implements and animals; for an artisan, loss of the tools of his trade; for a merchant, loss of his shop; for a

cleric, loss of his books; for a noble, loss of his horse and arms. Without these things a man ceased to be anything, because he no longer possessed the means to carry on a social existence. Stripped of his social position and excluded from the community, he was forced into emigration and vagabondage. The poor man was uprooted and alone." Mollat, p. 3.

3. p. 92 Deadheads would have been called Gueux in the Middle Ages. Hostile to the established order they lived in bands on the edge of society. "Recruited from the indigent population and living in indigence, these asocial individuals blackened the reputation of the "true" poor who shared their destitution." Mollet, p. 7

"In keeping with the logic of this conception of society, those who had no social function had no place in society. Some had withdrawn voluntarily from social life, others had been expelled. What placed these people outside the community was not poverty but marginality. Their only salvation was to reenter ordinary society. Given the context, however, it is not difficult to understand why, a century earlier, efforts to rehabilitate such people by men like Robert of Arbrissel and Fulk of Neuilly were considered by many to be aberrations as outrageous as the asocial or rebellious behavior of those whom they sought to save.

From the spiritual standpoint, however, things looked somewhat different. Poverty, like any form of suffering, had potential spiritual value. Through this spiritual function poverty recouped its standing and indeed found some justification: It could be useful to the pauper as well as the rich man, for whom it served as a means of sanctification. In some respects the sharing of poverty in the broad sense of the term grouped its victims into a sort of spiritual ordo, an ordo with no existence outside the economy of salvation, the communion of saints. The poor thus acquired a new social standing, and it is here, I think, that one finds the key to twelfth-century thinking and attitudes toward poverty and the poor.

Most authors apparently conceived of the poor man in terms of his relation to the rich man. The pauper would seem to have been created and placed in the world for the sake of the rich man's salvation. Men never tired of pointing out the reason why: it was more difficult for a rich man to enter the kingdom of heaven than for a camel to pass through the eye of a needle. The giving of alms became the subject of countless treatises, letters, and sermons. The primary function of the pauper was to receive, because it was a duty for the rich man to give. In theory as well as practice the twelfth-century reaffirmed the teaching of the ages, further analyzing, articulating, and extending the tradition in keeping with the twin principles of charity and justice." Mollat, p 106.

We now have a well-organized highly productive project to help the homeless-The Homeless Garden Project. Fifteen homeless gardeners are employed at the garden off Pelton, between Laguna and Lighthouse Avenue. They are paid minimum wage. The produce is sold at Farmers' Markets and is given to contributors to the project.

Will you help us and join our fund-raising drive?

YES! In order to help secure the future of the Homeless Garden Project, ☐ I agree to contribute $ 25.00 a month, to the Homeless Garden Project. I understand that my contribution is tax deductible.

☐ I agree to contribute $10 a month to the Homeless Garden Project. I understand that my contribution is tax deductible

_____

NAME

_____

ADDRESS

_____

CITY   STATE   ZIP

_____

TELEPHONE

An invoice for $10.00 or $25.00 will be sent monthly with an addressed and stamped return envelope.

Thank you for your support and for making the Homeless Garden Project your charity for 1992-93

COMMITTEE OF ONE HUNDRED
COMMITTEE OF ONE THOUSAND
THE HOMELESS GARDEN PROJECT

An affiliate of the Citizens Committee for The Homeless
A 501 C3 nonprofit corporation
2601 Park Avenue, Soquel, California 95073